Praise
The Art of War **...cutives**

"An interesting, insightful and fun book."
—*Small Business*

"Even after several thousand years, Sun Tzu's advice wears well."   —*Atlanta Business Chronicle*

"*The Art of War for Executives* saves the student or businessperson from having to mentally transfer Sun Tzu's instructions on how to wage war to how to successfully conduct a business . . . informative and helpful."
     —John B. McKinnon, Dean, Babcock Graduate
          School of Management, Wake Forest University

"The workplace has long been seen by some as a battleground, so why not take a more militant approach to your career? Now there's a field guide."
—*Akron Beacon Journal*

"This book's handy format is useful . . . Krause has preserved the character and tone of the original treatise."
—*The Columbus Dispatch*

"A wealth of ancient wisdom translated superbly for today's reader."   —*The European* (London)

THE WAY
OF THE
LEADER

Donald G. Krause

A Perigee Book

A Perigee Book
Published by The Berkley Publishing Group
200 Madison Avenue
New York, NY 10016

Copyright © 1997 by Donald G. Krause
Book design by Rhea Braunstein
Cover design by James R. Harris
Cover illustration by James Barkley

First edition: January 1997

Published simultaneously in Canada.

The Putnam Berkley World Wide Web site address is
http://www.berkley.com/berkley

Library of Congress Cataloging-in-Publication Data
Krause, Donald G.
    The way of the leader / Donald G. Krause.—1st ed.
        p.   cm.
    "A Perigee book."
    ISBN 0-399-52267-0
    1. Leadership.   2. Sun-tzu 6th cent. B.C.—Views on
    leadership.
3. Confucius—Views on leadership.   I. Title.
HD57.7.K73   1997
658.4'092—dc20   96-22371
                                                           CIP

Printed in the United States of America

10   9   8   7   6   5   4   3   2   1

In memory of
Evelyn Elizabeth McWilliams Bradshaw

Acknowledgments

I would like to thank the many people who helped me with encouragement and ideas. The perceptive comments of my American publisher, John Duff, greatly increased the value of this book for the reader. The support of my British publisher, Nicholas Brealey, helped me to keep focused on completing the task and planning for additional work. The efforts of my agents, Susan Urstadt and Jeanne Fredericks, have spread these books, for better or worse, across the entire world. The cultural insights of my good friend and valued associate Dr. Chang Miao, principal of the West Suburban Chinese Language School in the Chicago area, enhanced my understanding of the applications of oriental philosophy. Finally, I would like to thank Dr. Bob Shively of the Babcock Graduate School of Management at Wake Forest University for introducing me—a "real prickly son of a bitch," to quote Bob in 1975—to the possibility that it is the power of people in business that actually gets the job done.

Introduction

Understanding the nature of leadership and developing strong leadership skills is probably the single most important task for society today. Organizations and nations prosper or decline based solely on the vision and capability of their leaders. But the challenges of developing leaders are not new, nor are they unique to modern times. The rulers of ancient China also spent a great deal of time studying and thinking about leadership, particularly leadership under conditions of great difficulty—that is, the change, chaos, and uncertainty caused by war, famine, and social upheaval. The leadership concepts of two men in particular, the famous general Sun Tzu, and the great philosopher Confucius, when taken together, outline a system that has worked for centuries even under the worst possible conditions. The purpose of this book, *The Way of the Leader*, is to organize and integrate business-related adaptations of the concepts of these two men, along with the best ideas of modern military and political leaders, into a clear and understandable framework for effective leadership that can be used successfully by individuals and organizations in today's competitive international business environment.

Sun Tzu developed the fundamental concepts of success in warfare and competition that are found in his timeless book, *The Art of War*, about 2500 years ago. But, while Sun Tzu's classic text is still the definitive work on winning battles, its main focus is basic competitive strategy. Even the most enlightened strategy requires effective leadership in order to succeed. Sun Tzu himself emphasizes that success in competition depends largely, if not entirely, on the quality and strength of leadership. But in *The Art of War*, he does not give us a workable description of the characteristics of a capable leader.

Confucius lived at approximately the same time as Sun Tzu. Because they were near contemporaries, Confucian teachings can be used to provide us with reliable insight into the moral and philosophical foundations of Sun Tzu's ideas. Confucian teachings distill the prevailing sociological and ethical ideals of that time period, including the how and why of Sun Tzu's leadership and command principles. Confucian thoughts on leadership give us a doorway to using Sun Tzu's ideas and developing a more comprehensive understanding of successful leadership—particularly leadership under difficult and challenging conditions.

Confucian teachings come to us, in part, through a series of short lessons called analects. Modern translations of Confucius include approximately 450 analects. I have borrowed about 120 analects for use in this text. The selected Confucian teachings incorporated here deal only with leadership, competition, and power. Further, they have been extensively rewritten using modern business language so they relate directly to modern business situations.

The nature of leadership is a controversial topic that has spawned many theories about what constitutes capable leadership and how strong, effective leadership can be developed. The ideas contained in this book, of course, are not new. But, time and again over the last 2500 years, they have worked well. If you believe, like Sun Tzu, that success on both a corporate and a personal level is determined in large measure by acquiring and using leadership power, then these ideas can help you find the path to achievement. This book brings the philosophical vision of *The Art of War* and *The Analects of Confucius* to the bottom line. It is designed to be a schematic for victory; a road map to success. If you use the ideas of Sun Tzu and Confucius, in conjunction with good management practices, you can and will become a better, more powerful business leader!

The Difference Between Leadership and Management

This book is about business leadership. I believe that while leadership and management in business situations are certainly related to one another and are both required for overall success, there is a distinction between them. To me, leadership *requires* recognition of a social contract between the leader and his followers. The leader must possess both the *will* and the *ability* to control the outcomes of events through the cooperative exercise of power over the actions of other people. Further, the power to lead must be freely given by those being led. Leadership power is grounded in mutual consent, expectations, and commitment. Since management power is primarily derived from position or ownership, management does not necessarily require these factors in order to work. Management, depending on the situation, can be effective without recognition of a social contract between managers and employees, and without the agreement of those being managed. However, I think everyone would agree that the results of good management practices are enhanced and magnified through the complementary joining of management power with leadership power. The purpose of this book is to provide a framework for helping already good managers become effective leaders, too.

Organization of the Text

The text is organized into three sections. The first section, "Leadership Basics," is an introduction to the leadership philosophy of Sun Tzu and Confucius as it applies to business. The second section, "The SPARKLE Principles," contains seven chapters that guide you through the seven principles of leadership that work together to form the character of an ideal leader. These seven principles are: **S**elf-Discipline, **P**urpose, **A**ccomplishment, **R**esponsibility, **K**nowledge, **L**addership ("Laddership" is a word I coined to create a strong visual image. It is explained in detail later.), and **Ex**ample. The first letters of each principle taken together form the acronym **SPARKLE**.

The third section, "Lessons in Leadership," contains a series of anecdotal discussions about how famous leaders from more recent history successfully applied the principles revealed here to achieve personal and organizational success. The leaders covered in the series are George Washington, Robert E. Lee, Winston S. Churchill, Ulysses S. Grant, Thomas A. Edison, George C. Marshall, T. E. Lawrence, and Dwight D. Eisenhower.

You will quickly perceive that none of the people discussed in the third section is a modern "business" executive. I did not think I could adequately use modern business executives as examples of good leaders for this reason: At times, there can be considerable confusion about what constitutes outstanding leadership in the practice of organization management today. Many notable (or perhaps "notorious" would be a better word in some cases) modern executives are excellent showmen; many notable business successes come to the public's attention through effective public relations campaigns. Sometimes, in an environment of sensationalism, public recognition does not come from attaining worthwhile results. Great modern executive leaders may not, as a consequence, get the publicity they deserve. Because of this, my research was not able to uncover enough *trustworthy* and *reliable* information for me to objectively judge the ability or character of contemporary executives, particularly those whose names have become household words. As a result, I have chosen to discuss the exploits of historical leaders whose lives have been thoroughly documented. The accomplishments of the leaders discussed here have definitely not been created overnight by press releases. Further, the value of their efforts has truly passed the test of time.

To accomplish the purposes of *The Way of the Leader*, I gathered together relevant ideas found in ancient and modern texts, most notably Sun Tzu's *The Art of War* and Confucius's *The Analects of Confucius*. I organized and rewrote these ideas into an understandable format and reinterpreted them so they apply directly to modern business. I researched the lives and exploits of famous leaders to show how they applied the ideas discussed here to the situations they faced.

And, finally, I carefully defined each leadership principle so the reader can gauge his own behavior in relation to the definition and improve his performance, particularly performance in the business environment we face today.

In rewriting the passages used here, I have tried to retain the original flavor of the material while at the same time updating and arranging the prose for business readers. Since the passages used come from many different sources, they have been placed within the context of this book according to how well they fit the subject being discussed and how well they support the development of that subject.

Section I

LEADERSHIP BASICS

I
The Character of Leadership

Leadership can be defined as the will to control events, the understanding to chart a course, and the power to get a job done, cooperatively using the skills and abilities of other people. The goals and requirements of strong, effective leadership are the same now as they were 2500 years ago at the time of Sun Tzu and Confucius.

Sun Tzu and Confucius believed that leadership, at its most fundamental level, comes from within. The power to lead is generated within the context of a person's moral and philosophical framework in relation to one's followers and constituents . . . it is a function of character, not an accident of birth or a prerogative of position. The character of a strong leader can be developed only through careful, intentional practice. The substance of leadership can be glimpsed, but not learned, by attending two-day corporate seminars or two-week trips to the wilderness. For it to take hold, it must be ingested, digested, encouraged, and utilized over a long period of time. Further, the requirements of effective, profitable leadership under difficult business conditions—conditions involving rapid change, internal and external conflict, technological chaos, and political, sociological, and economic uncertainty—are challenging.

Sun Tzu, in *The Art of War*, says that competitive success (that is, success under conditions of change, conflict, chaos, and uncertainty such as are commonly found on the battlefield and, by extension, in a rapidly developing marketplace) is determined by leadership skill alone. He further states that leadership skill can be assessed in terms of several factors that derive from a person's character. Using the philosophy underlying the teachings of Confucius in *The Analects of Confucius*, I have identified seven factors that form the essence of leadership: **S**elf-Discipline, **P**urpose, **A**ccomplishment, **R**esponsibility, **K**nowledge, **L**addership, and **E**xample. I have termed these seven factors the SPARKLE Principles. Not only do the SPARKLE Principles provide the basic structure, or framework, for learning the ancient art of leadership as defined by Sun Tzu and Confucius, but (as you will see from the examples provided in section III) successful leaders throughout history have used them consistently to shape their lives and guide their decisions.

The SPARKLE Principles were developed with the idea that they would be used as a measure or gauge of the quality of leadership. The closer a person's behavior follows these principles, the stronger leader he becomes. Learning how to use the SPARKLE Principles in your job and in your life can make you a more effective leader and, as a result, a more powerful executive. Training executives to use them will give any organization a decided competitive advantage.

The SPARKLE Principles are defined as follows:

Self-Discipline means that a leader tends to live by a set of rules or principles that he determines are appropriate for him and acceptable to his constituents. A leader does not need external motivation to ensure performance.

Purpose means that a leader develops intense determination to achieve his vision and his objectives. Intense determination creates high morale and spirit among constituents. This allows the leader to effectively employ both personal and organizational power to accomplish goals. The leader uses this power to direct and control the efforts of his followers.

Accomplishment means that a leader defines results in terms of meeting the needs of his constituents. Successful results are the foundation of leadership. Taking effective action is the basis for successful results. The elements of effective action are decision, determination, energy, simplicity, balance, and chance.

Responsibility means that a leader embraces the duties and obligations that grow from the trust and power given him. The most critical of these obligations are clear perception, determined action, and an overriding concern for the best interests of his constituents. A strong leader owns up to the results of his decisions and actions and shares their consequences along with his constituents.

Knowledge is the foundation of successful leadership. Knowledge has three aspects. The first, *fundamental knowledge*, deals with studying science, history, and human nature; in other words, learning the basics of the art of leadership. The second, *strategic knowledge*, concerns understanding the needs and goals of both constituents and competitors and planning effective operations to reach objectives. The third, *tactical knowledge*, focuses on uncovering evolving threats and opportunities and responding swiftly and appropriately to them, within the strategic framework, through innovation and improvisation.

Laddership means that a leader understands the special nature of the social and moral contract between leaders and their constituents. The leader is dependent upon his followers for his power and, to a large extent, his ability to produce results. Therefore, he must work cooperatively with them to reach agreed-upon objectives. But, at the same time, strong leadership is one of the more important factors, if not the only absolutely necessary one, in the success of those human activities that depend upon cooperation. Therefore, a leader is charged with the responsibility of imposing, through the exercise of appropriate power, whatever level of order and discipline is required to meet objectives. He does this in part by using a system of rewards and penalties that is perceived as fair and just by his constituents.

I created the word "laddership" in order to provide a clear visual image. Imagine for a moment that you and your organization are climbing a tall ladder to reach your goals. You are in charge of getting the group to climb as quickly as possible; but all of you are on the ladder at the same time and, as a group, you must be careful not to make the ladder tip over. If one person succeeds, all succeed; if one person falls off, all fall off. Laddership implies the organization, communication, and cooperation that must exist in order for your ladder-climbing team to reach the top. If your team members do not work together effectively, that is, if they are not adequately organized, if they do not communicate with one another (and with you, their leader), and if they are unwilling to cooperate with one another and you, they will not succeed. If your team members use appropriate "laddership," it will mean a fast trip to the top of the ladder; if they use inappropriate "laddership," it will mean an even faster trip to the bottom.

Example means that a leader's actions become a model for the actions of his constituent group. Further, the leader's character sets the moral tone of leadership. The standards he uses become the benchmarks for the group. The people he favors become his flag-bearers. In all situations, the leader is observed and copied; at all times, the leader demonstrates preferred or ideal behavior by his own actions. The leader sets the example whether he intends to or not!

Let's take a closer look at why the SPARKLE Principles of Sun Tzu and Confucius are as important in winning the battles of business today as they were in winning the military campaigns of ancient China.

The Best Way to Get Things Done

The main goal of exercising the power of leadership is to accomplish useful and desirable things that benefit the people being led. For the last twenty-five years or so, I have been researching leaders and leadership with the idea of determining the "best way" for groups and organizations to get things done. It turns out that the "best way" to get things done can be distilled into one short, clear statement: **Do the essential things well**! But, as clear and simple (almost simplistic) as it sounds, "doing the essential things well" is extremely difficult in practice and requires a special kind of manager—a manager who is also a powerful, effective leader—in other words, a leader who "SPARKLES"!

This philosophy—Do the essential things well!—contains the three fundamental concepts that appear to govern the actions of the successful leaders discussed later, and which make up the essence of leadership according to Sun Tzu and Confucius. The three principles are:

1. Be Proactive. (**Do** through action.)
2. Reduce Complexity. (Concentrate effort on basic, critical tasks, the **essential** things.)
3. Seek Improvement. (Get the essential things done **better**!)

Why do these three ideas work so well in business? Business, like war or politics, is a series of situations, events, opportunities, threats, and crises. For the most part, success in business is a matter of profitably executing the same basic activities over and over again. Hence, at its most fundamental level, "doing the essential things well" makes business processes more profitable. It is unquestionably useful, perhaps even necessary, to create statements of corporate purpose and perform detailed, long-term strategic planning; but without sustained levels of profitable execution in critical day-to-day operations, purpose statements and strategic plans have little chance of success. (Vince Lombardi's coaching methods were based on "doing the essential things well." He said: "Our team only has a few simple plays. We practice them over and over again until we can execute them perfectly. The other teams know exactly what we are going to do; but we execute these plays so well, our opponents cannot stop us.")

All success in business can be reduced to completing critical tasks profitably. This may seem like an overstatement of the obvious, but the fact is that critical tasks must be finished, with the revenue from these tasks exceeding the cost incurred. Too often this fundamental purpose of business is lost in the maze of competing functions and procedures that have become part of the complex business process. In basketball, the object of the game is not to run up and down the court. The object is to score points. According to Sun Tzu, in war, the object is not to *destroy* lives and property. The object is to *win* as painlessly as possible. In the same vein, the object of business is not to create plans and spend money. The object is to earn a profit. Earning a profit depends less on *performing* tasks than it does on *completing* jobs effectively. This elementary truth can disappear in many organizations.

There is also a scientific basis for the belief that things work better if we "do the essential things well." To explain, let me introduce three interrelated concepts. Let's begin with a concept provided by W. Edwards Deming, one of the founders of the Total Quality Management (TQM) movement. Some of his best ideas have to do with understanding the relationship between complex processes and process optimization—in other words, the relationships involved in doing difficult, complex operations in the best possible way. Deming tells us that we can never know everything there is to know about a complex process. (Complex processes include, for example, not only the workings of the national economy or a good-sized business, but may also include interactions in a human group with more than just a handful of participants.) Further, he says the knowledge that we really need to optimize a complex process is unknowable. Therefore, we can only approach optimization a little at a time as our understanding grows; but we can never reach it in one big leap.

Deming implies from this that we should seek continuous improvement, but we are unrealistic when we seek absolute optimization. If we try to take big steps, we will lose the ability to predict or control the outcome of the actions we take. As a result, we can neither measure nor understand the impact of our improvement actions. We lose control. The outcomes of our actions become more random, and we cannot ascertain, for sure, the appropriate cause and effect relationships. This happens because large changes in already complex processes introduce even greater complexity. Greater complexity, in turn, *reduces* our ability to understand what is going on.

On the other hand, "doing the essential things well" reduces complexity and increases our ability to control and understand events. Controlling and understanding events, particularly those critical to our success, allows us to exercise more effective leadership. I believe Dr. Deming, Sun Tzu, and Confucius would have agreed on many points. This may perhaps explain why Deming was so successful in helping Japan rebuild its manufacturing base after World War II.

The second of the three concepts deals with process improvement from another viewpoint. The question raised in the paragraph above is: If we cannot wholly understand how a complex process works, then how is it possible to improve it? One way to successfully approach improving complex processes is by reducing the scope of our actions to understanding and controlling those parts of the process that have the most impact on critical outcomes of the process. We can do this by applying Pareto's Law, or the 80/20 Principle, that states that about 20 percent of the inputs to a process cause or influence about 80 percent of the outputs. Among other things, this principle is used in Total Quality Management programs to do root-cause analysis. By applying the 80/20 Principle, it is possible to improve complex processes by focusing attention on that 20 percent of the process that more heavily impacts the outcomes we want to improve, for example, profitability or error rate. Doing the essential things well allows us to focus rapidly on those activities that may benefit from improvement. Rapid, constant focus on critical operational elements is necessary for process improvement. But maintaining focus requires strong leadership.

The third concept is concerned with probabilities and reality. We are a "cause and effect" society. We are taught that every event, every outcome, every result must have a definite, explainable cause and/or a definite, identifiable hero or culprit. When things go well, somebody or something (perhaps everybody) claims the credit. When things go poorly, somebody or something must get the blame. This highly deterministic view of reality is truly dysfunctional when applied to complex processes that are constantly evolving in an infinite number of ways. In complex processes, no one knows for sure why things happen or what will happen next.

According to Deming, no one can ever know for sure. Under the conditions of uncertainty that exist in the real world, when we try something, the best we can do is assign probabilities to the possible outcomes. Or, conversely, given a definite outcome (for instance, the stock market goes down, a train accident occurs), we can only assign probabilities to possible causes. Assigning probabilities, rather than blame, keeps failure in perspective and encourages people to take calculated risks. Failure must be expected at times; in fact, given enough tries, failure is inevitable. (Fortunately for many of us, so is success . . . given enough tries!) By using probabilities, however, failure does not become the final word. If a controllable or identifiable factor caused the failure, we can learn from it. If no cause is apparent, then the failure resulted from something we do not yet understand. No one is blamed without reasonable evidence of cause and effect.

The major objective of leadership, then, is to do the essential things well. By doing the essential things well, we manage realistically each of the three concepts presented above. First, doing the essential things well reduces the level of complexity of our actions, making it easier to understand what impact our actions have on subsequent outcomes. Second, since the essential things are fewer in number, they are easier to separate into critical and not-so-critical groups. We can manage our activities better. Third, probabilities associated with essential things can be assessed more accurately. Whether failure or success occurs, post-action analysis of important elements can yield more information about improving processes further and about the relationship among factors. Warren Bennis put this concept succinctly when he said, "The job of leaders is not necessarily to do things right. The job of leaders is to do the right things!" By using the SPARKLE Principles, executives have a clear, concise model for meeting the challenge of doing the essential things well!

Leadership Under Difficult Conditions

A great deal of attention has been focused in recent years on theories and systems designed to make companies run more effectively. We do not need another theory about how to manage in general so much as we need a better understanding of the requirements of management under difficult conditions—that is, under conditions of change, conflict, chaos, and uncertainty. Management under difficult conditions requires, in addition to high-level technical skills, a great commitment to the moral and philosophical elements of character, an emphasis that has been lacking up until now in the training of most managers. Those of us who have had a classical management education were trained to think analytically. We were trained to believe that planning solves most problems, and things should happen in accordance with the way they are planned. Hence, managers have become enamored of systematic, organized management paradigms such as Total Quality Management and corporate reengineering. We can see them; we can feel them; we can understand them; we can spend enormous amounts of time and money on them. Unfortunately, at times, we cannot seem to make them work as well as we think they should!

Why don't these carefully crafted systems work? First, in practice, they are too complicated; that is, they do not concentrate attention on doing the essential and critically important tasks better. Second, they leave out consideration of the critical importance of the underlying human element (even though there is *always* a great deal of discussion about considering the human element). In some cases, failure can occur because the contribution of leadership power is underestimated; in others, because the plan or the system becomes a weak substitute for real leadership. (On this subject, General George Patton once said: "Battles are won by great execution, not by great plans! Great execution can save a mediocre plan; poor execution will always ruin a great plan.")

The solution to the problem of rapidly improving products and services is putting more emphasis on combining management power with leadership power. Everyone agrees that organizations must evolve as competitive conditions change. But effective management of planned evolution is particularly difficult to accomplish, because people seem to resist it with great tenacity. Resistance to evolution occurs because evolution involves change, and change is frightening. Fear of change is necessary for individual survival be cause, at an individual level, change may cause harm. But evolutionary change is often necessary for group survival. Even radical change may be required at times.

This is obvious in the natural world. Observe how certain species of plants and animals have come into being in response to favorable conditions, flourished for a time in those conditions, and then, for the most part, died off when conditions changed. Species that survive in the long run (for example, sharks, cockroaches, and crocodiles) are those that are able to adapt to changes in environmental conditions. What nature does by accident, organizational leadership must do on purpose, through effective use of leadership power, regardless of how frightened the individual members of the organization might be.

My favorite example of survival through adaptation is the lowly ant. Ants have been around for 250 million years virtually unchanged. Why? First, they do the essential things well. That is, they have an uncomplicated organizational structure based on unified leadership and highly trained and motivated personnel. (All of this, of course, accomplished through genetic programming.) Further, they have an efficient strategy for meeting physical needs based on never-ending, low-cost searches for profitable opportunities. Finally, they are masters of communication and execution. Ants adapt when their environment changes, through their willingness to search and experiment within existing environmental conditions to get what they need. (Amazingly, scientists have identified thousands of different species of ants living today. It is estimated that there are at least five times as many species that we have not yet identified.) Any organization can do the same thing by using the same techniques: that is, conducting large numbers of low-cost experiments; improving training programs; motivating people; establishing clear communication; and promoting quick execution—all of which, according to Sun Tzu and Confucius (and, not surprisingly, Tom Peters, too!), are the really important functions of effective leadership under difficult conditions.

Resistance to change also occurs because, even when everyone finally agrees that change is necessary, not everyone will agree on the magnitude and direction of the change required. This is where probabilistic, rather than deterministic, thinking helps. The results of changing a complex process are never completely predictable in advance. All we can do is estimate reasonable probabilities about what may happen. Further, if we emphasize leadership and execute a number of simple strategies designed to provide information rapidly about what works and what does not work, rather than betting everything on one approach, particularly an approach that may require a long time to work (such as TQM or reengineering), we increase our chances of getting useful information and succeeding overall.

Solutions to the problem of implementing the required changes are abundant. The business media and management experts are constantly formulating new and useful approaches. But, as discussed above, these approaches do not always work as well as they could.

A great deal of well-intentioned activity often takes place. Time and effort, not to mention money, is often spent. People are trained, reorganized, and exhorted, but improvements that would justify these expenditures of time and effort do not always happen. Certain Total Quality Management (TQM) programs are, at times, good examples of this phenomenon. So is corporate reengineering.

Corporate reengineering became a hot topic in 1993 when Michael Hammer and James Champy published their book, *Reengineering the Corporation*. After explaining the benefits of their idea for thirteen chapters, the authors begin chapter fourteen with the following paragraph:

> "*Sadly*, we must report that despite the success stories described in previous chapters, many companies that begin reengineering don't succeed at it. They end their efforts precisely where they began, making no significant changes, achieving no major performance improvement, and fueling employee cynicism with yet another ineffective business improvement program. Our unscientific estimate is that as many as *50 percent to 70 percent* of the organizations that undertake a reengineering effort do not achieve the dramatic results they intended." (emphasis added)

Hammer and Champy suggest a cause for these costly failures:

"Most reengineering failures stem from breakdowns in leadership. Without strong, aggressive, committed, and knowledgeable leadership, there will be no one to . . . *convince* the people affected by reengineering that no alternative exists and that the results will be worth the *agony* of the process." (emphasis added)

Another pair of authors believe reengineering failures occur because corporate management in the last several decades has not had a clear framework for integrating high-level management skills with the leadership power necessary to deal with the challenge of managing change successfully. Daniel P. Petrozzo and John C. Stepper make the following observation in their book, *Successful Reengineering*:

"Few members of the upper management of most companies have reached their position because of their competence and hard-driving, uncompromising desire to do things right. In many cases, their climbing the corporate ladder . . . resulted from consensus building, networking, and the ability to make any project seem like a success. The leader of a reengineering team must have the qualities that one would expect all senior managers to have . . ."

By implication, then, Petrozzo and Stepper believe that senior corporate executives succeed in reaching their positions because they build consensus (they are good team players and understand how to manipulate situations), they network (they communicate well and have good social skills), and they make themselves look successful (they have an appropriate image and effective public relations). These qualities are, of course, highly desirable qualities for any executive, regardless of level, to possess.

So what's the problem? The problem is that there appears to be another element, in addition to highly developed management skills, that is required for the job of successful change management. (In a magazine article, Tom Peters put it bluntly, but correctly: "It's leadership, stupid!" He went on to say that a mediocre organization with good leadership is generally effective, while a superior organization with poor leadership is not.) Consensus building, networking, and image manipulation are critical political skills. But based on historical success and failure rates for major change projects, political skills are not sufficient. This is not to say that political skills are not appropriate (and necessary) in most business situations. But another factor needs to be combined with political skills in situations that introduce unstable and unpredictable conditions, including, for instance, implementing corporate reengineering or TQM projects. The missing factor is the ability to use leadership power in conjunction with management skills.

Petrozzo and Stepper imply that organizations may not have a framework for developing executives who are strong in critical situation skills. Without an understanding of how to use leadership power, people who are good at everyday management may not be so good at crisis management. But if an organization is going to take advantage of the profit possibilities inherent in change and evolution, it will need executives with both kinds of skills. Is this possible? Dynamic, aggressive problem-solvers with highly developed human relations skills! Subtle, sophisticated networkers who get the job done! How can it happen? It happens by applying the SPARKLE leadership principles of Sun Tzu and Confucius.

Task Levels, Structure, and Responsibility

Let's expand this discussion by differentiating task levels within an organization to provide a systematic framework for talking about structure and responsibility.

Imagine that tasks involved in handling people and running an organization fall along a continuum. At one end of the continuum are tasks that are primarily *caretaking*. These tasks involve applying fairly rigid policies to standard situations. *Caretakers* do not have the authority to make decisions, nor are they able to create change. They learn to follow policy and precedent. If a caretaker encounters a situation that requires a decision outside of established policy, he must request that decision from a person who is farther along the continuum.

In the center of the continuum are tasks that are *supervisory*. These tasks involve limited decisions about how to implement assigned tasks using budgeted resources. Generally, *supervisors* must follow policy. Supervisors rely heavily on precedent. Supervisors generally cannot institute change because they also lack the requisite authority. They can resolve difficulties in policy or precedent interpretation for caretakers and subordinate supervisors, but only within the narrow range of activity and budgets assigned to them.

At the far end of the continuum are *command* tasks. These tasks involve responsibility for determining both the direction of effort and the allocation of resources for significant parts of the organization. *Commanders* alone have the authority to institute organizational change, because organizational change is in effect a reallocation of organizational focus and resources. Commanders cannot rely on precedent, because precedent in rapidly evolving situations does not exist, except in a general sense. The task of command is the task of determining appropriate objectives, allocating resources, and then achieving objectives. People who are responsible for command tasks must possess vision and drive, imagination and persistence, in order to succeed. In short, commanders must be leaders. Because organization survival ultimately depends on the decisions and character of those in command, Sun Tzu tells us that strong leaders are an organization's most vital resource.

Leaders may be a scarce commodity because, as we noted above, a clear, usable framework for developing and using leadership power in managers and caretakers may not have existed. As a result, leaders have not always had an opportunity to develop in an organization until a crisis occurs and it is almost too late. (As an example of this phenomenon, look at what General George C. Marshall needed to do with the leadership of the U.S. military at the beginning of World War II. Virtually every general officer on active duty in the army at the beginning of 1939 had to be replaced.) The ability and competence of leadership must develop before challenging conditions occur. It appears, however, that the quality and quantity of leadership required has not always been available when it was needed. Further, without a simple, understandable framework for developing leadership, it is easy to see why there is often a shortage of effective leaders.

All executives who are assigned to lead organizational change projects must be trained in command and leadership skills if these projects are to have a realistic chance of success. This is because change projects are ambiguous. They cannot be neatly executed; hence, they are difficult and frustrating for untrained caretakers, supervisors, and managers to deal with. Deming says that we cannot know everything we need to know about any given complex process and that most of the really important information probably cannot be known at all. This leads to the conclusion that no matter how much time is spent planning beforehand, change projects develop a life of their own. Their success depends almost entirely on the ability of the change project leader to adapt the project's plans, methods, timetables, and even goals to experience gained during the attempt to implement the original strategy. This kind of adaptation is impossible for someone who has not been trained to lead under conditions of chaos and ambiguity. Count Helmuth von Moltke, Chief of Staff of the Prussian Army during the mid-nineteenth century and formulator of basic German military strategy for World Wars I and II, said: "No plan of operations extends with certainty beyond the first encounter with the enemy. Only the layman sees in the course of a campaign a consistent execution of a preconceived and highly detailed original concept pursued to the end."

An effective leader is a person who brings people together in response to challenges, melds them into cohesive units, develops strategies for overcoming challenges, and executes the strategies successfully. An effective leader is neither abrasive nor abusive, overbearing nor overwhelming. The chief characteristic of an effective leader is the ability to really get the job done without destroying the people on his, or anyone else's, team. (This follows Sun Tzu's comment that the best generals win the war without fighting.) Organizations that systematically select, train, and nurture people with these leadership and command skills have **the critical advantage**.

Remaking an organization is risky and problematic. This is already apparent from the failure rate of TQM and reengineering projects. Perhaps these projects do not succeed because the very ingredient, the very people, necessary for their success may not be available in the senior positions in an organization at the time they are needed. If we are sincerely seeking answers to real problems that are impacting our ability to succeed at rejuvenating organizations, it is easy to put our faith in organized and logical ideas or methods for success— such as TQM or reengineering. And indeed, given the right people, the right leaders, these programs can make major contributions. But in many cases they fail . . . not through lack of effort, investment, or talent, but through lack of training in, and understanding of, leadership.

Success in organizations depends not on systems, but on people. Organizations succeed because people with the necessary skills and character occupy critical command positions at the right time. This has been true throughout history. Nations rise and fall based on the quality, competence, and character of their leaders. So do organizations. It is a great deal less expensive, and far less risky, to develop people with appropriate leadership skills, or to develop those skills in yourself, than to go through the agony of a TQM or reengineering project that has a high probability of failure because otherwise effective and capable executives do not have these skills. Developing leadership potential through appropriate training and philosophy creates value far out of proportion to the investment required. Further, developing the skills necessary to exercise command effectively under the chaotic and stressful conditions imposed by the current global marketplace, without destroying the organizational community, is a key to competitive success. It is the only way to guarantee future prosperity—on a personal level, on an organizational level, and on a global level. The SPARKLE Principles are an effective model for successful leaders.

Section II

THE SPARKLE PRINCIPLES

II

Self-Discipline

Self-Discipline: A leader tends to live by a set of rules or principles that he determines are appropriate for him and acceptable to his constituents. A leader does not need external motivation to ensure performance.

II-1
Self-discipline is the basic ingredient of self-control and the foundation of self-respect. If an executive lacks self-discipline, self-control, or self-respect, even if he is the person in charge, he will not, in fact, be the leader.

II-2
There are three steps necessary for an executive to gain the qualifications required to lead. Each step requires self-discipline.

II-3

The first step is self-determination. Every great leader goes through the process of self-determination. During this process, a leader determines what group he intends to lead and the rules and behaviors required by that group.

II-4

The second step is decision. A leader must decide to accept the rules and behaviors required, regardless of what anyone else thinks and, more importantly, regardless of the consequences.

II-5

The third step is action. The leader must act in a manner which is consistent with the required rules and behaviors. If a leader successfully completes these three steps, he can be confident in his position and enjoy the support of the group he intends to lead. But do not delude yourself. A real leader "walks the walk," or he cannot really lead. An executive may fool his superiors for a time, but he will not fool his subordinates.

II-6

Consider these three steps carefully. Can you see how it is possible for highly disciplined people who are thieves, scoundrels, or worse, to become powerful leaders? If a person follows the three steps, he can and will become a leader. He can and will exercise power. But exercising leadership power without morality is certainly dangerous.

II-7

In a very real sense, leaders not only control and direct their followers, they also personify the most significant characteristics of their groups. If you intend to lead, you must embrace your followers and their characteristics, both desirable and undesirable, otherwise your followers will not embrace you. Choose your followers carefully; you will become one with them!

II-8

Self-discipline means, at its most personal level, that you do not attempt to deceive yourself. Always be careful what you think and do, but be particularly careful when you believe you are alone. Practice self-restraint in your private life. Remember that a person's opinion of himself eventually shows in his face and is reflected in his outward behavior. A true leader exercises self-discipline through controlling his thoughts and actions even when he believes that no one else can see him.

II-9

Self-deception is particularly insidious because it destroys self-respect. Self-respect is fundamental to gaining the trust of your followers. And the trust of your followers is the true foundation of power.

II-10

The world is full of difficulties and trials. You probably will not find a person who does not have some faults, nor will you be without them yourself. What you can strive for, though, is to be the kind of person who, through self-discipline, remains faithful to his own principles.

II-11

In order to do this, no matter where you are, imagine that you see your principles surrounding you like loyal servants. If you keep them before you in this way, they will never forsake you.

II-12

Eating plain food; drinking cool, fresh water; resting in the sunshine—a person can find comfort in these simple things if he chooses. Wealth and rank, on the other hand, bring little comfort if acquired at the cost of self-respect.

II-13

A person without self-respect does not learn much from failure, nor does he benefit long from good fortune.

II-14

You will find that the consequences of strong ambition can, at different times in life, produce both joy and sorrow. A wise leader understands he cannot be first in every contest. Therefore, guard your emotions. Temper your actions. In times of good fortune, do not dissipate your gains. In times of sorrow, do not indulge in self-pity.

II-15
An effective leader exhibits a poised, self-assured, direct, and controlled demeanor under all circumstances. A controlled manner bestows powerful competitive advantages.

II-16
Above all, an effective leader is dignified without being arrogant. Arrogance comes from ignorance and lack of self-confidence. When a person displays arrogance, he is confirming that he knows very little about true dignity and, more importantly, very little about true leadership.

II-17
Practice the manner of the refined, not that of the masses. Do not indulge in bragging, pettiness, or other excessive behavior.

II-18
Few men will admit their own failures; and even fewer will acknowledge that the true cause of failure lies within themselves. But a person who practices self-discipline and continuously develops his level of skill seldom fails in the long term.

II-19

An effective leader worries about his own shortcomings and seeks improvement from within. When a person demands excellence from others, but never corrects problems within himself, he cannot lead.

II-20

Do not worry that others have failed to appreciate your talents; worry that you have not yet discovered and eliminated your own faults. Further, to recognize your own faults without working to eliminate them is truly wrong.

II-21

To know what is right and not to do it is an act of cowardice! Ignorance and fear are the roots of cowardice. Ignorance and fear destroy self-respect.

II-22

When an ignorant person makes an error, he will try to cover it up and blame someone else. For this reason, it can be difficult to work closely with ignorant people. They should not be placed in positions of power. When a person is aware of his own lack of true ability and is afraid to improve, he will stop at nothing to avoid being blamed for failure.

II-23

Be especially wary of bold, ignorant people who covet power! They are capable of using extreme methods. If their efforts are opposed, they will cause trouble.

II-24

There is no reason to follow someone who talks about leadership but is unwilling to pay the price for it. Few people are willing to demand excellence from themselves. A person who preaches excellence but practices mediocrity is no better than a common liar.

II-25

Study widely; inquire sincerely; adhere steadfastly to your principles; consider carefully your experiences, what works and what does not work for you. It is in doing these things that you will discover the meaning of excellence. Moreover, find the best leaders and copy their methods. In this way, you will also discover the meaning of leadership.

II-26

Excellence in leadership or anything else is not something remote or even difficult to find. We need only practice self-discipline, and it will begin to appear in our lives!

III
Purpose

Purpose: A leader develops intense determination to achieve his vision and his objectives. Intense determination creates high morale and spirit among constituents. This allows the leader to effectively employ both personal and organizational power to accomplish goals. The leader uses this power to direct and control the efforts of his followers.

III-1
What can be successfully accomplished must first be clearly seen and understood.

III-2
Therefore, the path to command starts with purpose. That is, resolve to do your best for those to whom you owe a duty. Give your superiors the same loyalty and service you expect from your subordinates.

III-3
Employees gain from associating with executives who have purpose and lose from associating with those who lack it. A world-class woodcarver who wants to create a masterpiece must first sharpen his tools. In seeking excellence, sharpen your intellect first by associating with those whose purpose is also to seek excellence.

III-4
Employees invariably reflect the attitude of their executive. The leader sets the tone. His spirit and his ability are naturally communicated to those who follow. There is an ancient saying: If you want to win a battle, it is better to have an army of asses commanded by a lion than an army of lions commanded by an ass.

III-5
Therefore, do not spend much time with an executive who states his good intentions, but does not take action to make them real. Many people talk readily about good intentions; but talk, by itself, does nothing. A person must take action to become a commander. Action is preceded by determination. And determination by purpose. Further, an executive's real value is no greater than the depth of his purpose. After all, a thoroughbred is not valued so much for his physical strength, but rather for his determined spirit.

III-6

Purpose manifests itself through self-discipline, reliability, and knowledge; lack of purpose in laxness, cleverness, and superficiality. Fast talk and arrogant behavior are seldom combined with sincerity of purpose.

III-7

An effective leader concentrates on overcoming difficulties, completing tasks, and obtaining desirable results. He thinks about the rewards of success after success has been attained.

III-8

A person makes enemies when his purpose is governed solely by self-interest and expediency. It is shortsighted to seek only money as a reward for performing services. When you are employed by someone, do your best. Regard the quality of your services as far more important than the amount of your compensation.

III-9

An effective executive displays neither greed nor pretense. Instead, he works diligently and speaks cautiously. He associates with those who value accomplishment in order to learn from them.

III-10

Purpose is the motivating force for achievement. When you are doing something which serves your purpose, you are at your best. A man cannot use what he learns without the fire of purpose in his heart. The driving ambition of sincere purpose alone enables him to perform great accomplishments.

III-11

To seek what is right rather than to accept what is easy; to show courage and patience in times of crisis; to honor legitimate obligations even when they become difficult or expensive—these actions are true reflections of purpose. Further, do your best for those who employ you. Keep faith with them. Befriend those who, like you, seek excellence. When you make a mistake, correct it.

III-12

An effective leader does not worry about being promoted. He worries about the quality and value of his work. An effective leader does not seek recognition; he seeks the opportunity to provide better service.

III-13

An effective executive must, of course, be intelligent, knowledgeable, and experienced. But strength of purpose and self-discipline are decisive factors in the competitive marketplace. The confidence of the people around him is based upon an executive's strength of purpose.

III-14

A leader should have a deep understanding of human nature and develop the ability to smooth out differences of opinion. He should have the power to gain affection while at the same time communicating urgency. He should possess the capacity for determined action at all times, and ruthless dedication when it is necessary. He needs to generate intense energy, but always keep a cool head. The greatest asset a capable executive can have is a controlled temperament. A controlled temperament bestows a sort of divine power, and it is only by means of divine power that you can motivate employees to peak performance in times of crisis.

III-15

When employees forge ahead and dare not slow down their efforts, this means they are more afraid of disappointing their own leaders than they are of being overworked.

III-16

An effective executive diligently seeks excellence in himself. When dealing with others, however, he is neither inflexible nor intolerant, particularly in matters of small importance.

III-17

If an executive is filled with purpose and if he pursues excellence with courage and determination, he will overcome all challenges.

III-18

An effective leader shows depth of purpose in five ways:

1. Tact and diplomacy
2. Tolerance for ambiguity
3. Reliability and loyalty
4. Diligence and quality
5. Regard for others

III-19

It is the responsibility of the leader to remain firm and constant in his decisions; he must show neither elation in prosperity nor depression in adversity.

III-20

Remaining firm and constant in decision is fundamental to gaining a reputation for purpose, because it allows your words to be relied on by others. As long as your actions do not create injustice, keep to your decisions. But remember that decisions made without thinking are often expensive.

III-21

The leader triggers the spirit and fires the imagination of his constituents.

III-22

The competition is won or lost in the mind of the leader. The outcome of competition depends on the judgment, the skill, and the courage of the executive in charge.

III-23

As a leader, you must watch your own morale and confidence level carefully. The business marketplace is, in effect, a never-ending contest of willpower and courage—your own versus that of the competition. If your confidence fails you when the issue hangs in the balance, the competition will win.

III-24

Listen carefully. Discard what cannot be proven and cautiously repeat the rest. Then your words will be correct. Observe closely. Ignore what does not work and judiciously employ the rest. Then your actions will be effective. When your words are correct and your actions are effective, then opportunities for power and command follow naturally.

III-25

Confidence, spirit, and attitude flow down the organization from those at the top and permeate the entire group. So do anxiety and lack of resolution.

III-26

Competitive victory is not possible unless the leader is energetic, bold, innovative, and eager for responsibilities; unless he possesses and can impart to his followers the will to see things through and to complete tasks; and unless he is capable of exercising good judgment, freedom of mind, and personal force in the midst of intense activity and competitive pressure.

III-27

In business, an effective executive is neither in favor of, nor opposed to, any particular idea or action until he has studied its purpose and effect. All other considerations aside, however, the truly effective leader supports the truth in whatever form he finds it. This requires courage combined with perception.

III-28

Courage and perception are the very qualities that inspire great achievement. In courage we will find safety because it requires courage to achieve the extraordinary. If we intend to reach great heights, we must dare to do great things. Courageous decisions can give the best chance of success. If a leader is courageous, he seizes opportunity without hesitating. But when perception is combined with courage, he also attracts allies because people are not afraid to follow.

III-29

An effective executive pursues truth; an ignorant person pursues short-term gains. An effective executive respects the spirit of rules and regulations; an ignorant person looks for loopholes and shortcuts.

III-30

An effective executive strives to discover what is right and then does it. An ignorant person simply does what is expedient, whether it is right or not.

III-31

Business success results from acting with vigor, decision, and confidence; one must not grope nor hesitate. In deciding to move, there can be no vacillation or indecision. Any vacillation will result in greater expense, loss of opportunity, and general discouragement. True wisdom for a leader is in vigorous execution once decisions are made. But maintain discipline and caution. Above all things, be on the alert for opportunity.

III-32

The surest way for an organization to succeed is to remain highly focused—that is, to be animated by one spirit, one mind, one purpose. Where there is no one in command, nothing useful or profitable will be completed. In business, it is disciplined effort that makes employees feel valuable and effective. Lack of unity and direction has destroyed many organizations. In business, order leads to profit.

III-33

Disciplined effort is the soul of accomplishment. It makes small companies formidable. Good order and disciplined effort in any company are to be depended upon more than assets. The firmness required for maintaining a tight competitive focus can only be obtained by a constant course of disciplined effort.

III-34

Motivate employees by depriving them of all means of distinction except through success. This is certainly the best method of making them produce, because real distinction can only be earned by passing a true test of performance.

III-35

The love of distinction, the ardent desire for recognition through achievement, is among the most potent and elevating of motives. The desire for distinction clings to men longer than any other passion. A truly worthwhile person does not sacrifice himself year after year for a few dollars of pension or some petty award. You must speak to his soul in order to motivate him.

III-36

It may be that the best executives possess superior intellects; they may be great marketers or financiers, but that is not their dominant characteristic. The best executives owe their successes to unstoppable purpose and tremendous energy.

III-37

Executive leadership requires, above all, purpose, intelligence, and empathy. Purpose is needed to motivate people to high-level achievement; intelligence, because people will only respect and willingly follow an executive who knows his profession thoroughly; and empathy, in order to understand each individual and draw out the best that is in him.

III-38

The force of purpose rather than numbers decides who wins the contest. Business today requires cohesion and unity more than at any previous time. It is not assets nor technology that brings profit. It is when one side uses the power of purpose that their competition cannot withstand them.

III-39

Purpose creates a determined state of mind. Determination results in steadfastness and courage and faith. It creates confidence and zeal and loyalty. It assures staying power and the will to win. An organization without purpose is nothing. With it, all things become possible.

III-40

It is not enough to be competent and effective. It is the spirit which we bring to the fight that decides the outcome. It is spirit that wins. Spirit is the greatest single factor in success. It is that intangible force which will move a whole group of people to give their last ounce to achieve something, without counting the cost to themselves; which makes them feel they are part of something greater than themselves.

III-41

Achieving constructive results requires more than intellect; it requires energy, drive, and unrelenting purpose, regardless of personal interests. Academic executives look on business as a purely intellectual exercise. They demand energy and commitment from the workforce, but not from themselves. Regarding themselves as the sole source of competitive wisdom, they rest content on their MBA's and professional qualifications . . . qualifications granted them by those of the same ilk. Only those with passion and purpose produce extraordinary results.

IV

Accomplishment

Accomplishment: A leader defines results in terms of meeting the needs of his constituents. Successful results are the foundation of leadership. Taking effective action is the basis for successful results. The elements of effective action are decision, determination, energy, simplicity, balance, and chance.

IV-1
Making good music is really quite simple. Begin with a composition which is appropriate for the time and place. Gather suitable instruments and capable artists. Meld them together into a coordinated unit with training and practice. Then, when the curtain goes up, make sure the score is performed from start to finish in harmony, with each musician playing his notes clearly at the proper time.

IV-2

In a contest of archery, the person with the strongest bow and the straightest arrow is not necessarily the one who triumphs. The person who succeeds is the one who hits the center of the target most often. Further, in the sport of archery, if you miss the target, it matters little whether you shoot over it or shoot under it.

IV-3

The goal of an effective executive is to succeed in meeting the needs of his constituents. Organizations cannot afford to keep a person who does not succeed. It is no use saying, "I am doing my best." A leader must accomplish what is necessary. The basic ideology of a leader can be summed up this way: When the chips are down, the main question is not how you go about meeting your objectives, but whether you succeed in doing so.

IV-4

The test of any leader lies in action, not in words. An effective leader does not overstate the promise of success for fear of disappointing others. He is slow to speak, but quick to act. He watches carefully over his words. It is a grave error to promise more than you can deliver.

IV-5

It is difficult to find all the qualities of a great executive combined in one person. What is most desirable is the balance of intelligence and ability with character and determination. If determination is predominant, the executive will attempt actions which are beyond his ability to complete successfully; if intellect is predominant, he will not dare to attempt his ideas.

IV-6
Success is gained only with vigor, decision, and unshaken determination; one must not grope or hesitate. The real leader displays his quality by winning over adversity, however great it may be.

IV-7
Action has three stages: (1) a decision to act based on analysis of the situation; (2) planning and preparation for action; and (3) the action itself. All three stages are influenced by the leader's determination. The ability to act is rooted in determination, and for an effective leader, determination is more important than intellect. Intellect without determination is ineffective; but determination without intellect can be dangerous.

IV-8
There is always the danger of loss in competitive activity, but we must decide between the possible loss of inaction and the rewards and risks of action. The essential factor in decision making is understanding the necessity to act at the right time.

IV-9

A leader who understands the risks inherent in making decisions in critical situations, especially when those decisions must be made under the pressure of great responsibility and in the midst of a thousand uncertainties and contradictions, will appreciate that most decisions cannot be made without some doubts. Even after a decision has been made, what may seem like a simple action often cannot be executed without great determination.

IV-10

Conceiving plans is the easiest part of effective action. Therefore, be cautious and take your time in making plans. But once you come to a decision, carry it out without hesitation or timidity. Timidity is not born of healthy caution, but is the stepchild of cowardice.

IV-11

Planning must be followed by effective execution. Execution is a matter of energy and initiative. What an executive needs most is a balanced combination of practical intellect and energy. Whatever is planned must be carried through. The executive should understand that just as much energy is required of him as mental ability. Sensational success is, more often than not, a triumph of energy rather than of intellect.

IV-12
No real success is possible unless an organization's executives are energetic, eager for responsibilities, and decisive; unless they can impart the will to see things through to profitable completion; and unless they are capable of exercising determination, good judgment, and control of emotion under pressure.

IV-13
The mark of an effective executive is the ability to maintain calm courage during a crisis. Inferior executives, on the other hand, are likely to attempt extreme or unwise measures. A good executive not only sees the way to success; he also knows when success is not possible. Thus it is said: "The path to victory may be known, but the time is not right!"

IV-14
Perfection is the enemy of effectiveness. An effective plan executed now is better than a perfect plan executed next quarter or next year. Success in most situations is determined by self-confidence, energy, and determination. These characteristics do not necessarily produce perfect solutions, but they can certainly produce profitable ones.

IV-15
Energy manifests itself primarily in mental agility. Mental agility allows an executive to seize opportunities and

to exploit unforeseen advantages in competitive, chaotic, and uncertain situations. Mental agility is the product not only of the executive's training and natural ability, but also his morale and initiative.

IV-16

Improvisation is the essence of mental agility, just as initiative is the outward indication of the power of decision. The ability to improvise is one of the main pillars of successful leadership. In competitive situations, improvisation surprises and disarms the competition. Always think ahead. Peek around corners. Spy out the heart of a problem. Serve your constituents in a manner that will astonish and delight them; this is effective improvisation. This is the foundation of successful leadership.

IV-17

Bold decisions give the best promise of success. But one must differentiate between a bold decision and a pure gamble. The outcome of a bold decision may not be success, but failure leaves one with sufficient resources to cope with whatever situation may arise. A pure gamble, on the other hand, is a decision which can lead either to complete success or to complete failure. Even a gamble may (and sometimes must) be justified, however, but only when circumstances leave no other choice.

IV-18

Success is composed of nothing more than taking advantage of accidents, and, although holding to sound management principles, an executive should never lose the opportunity to profit from one of these accidents; that is the mark of genius. In competitive business situations, there is always at least one favorable moment; the great skill is to recognize it and to seize it.

IV-19

The uncertain nature of business decisions requires assessing probabilities. Success resides in the realm of chance. Chance makes outcomes uncertain and constantly interferes with the workings of careful planning.

IV-20

In business situations, particularly under competitive or uncertain conditions, indecision and confusion are normal. Late, incomplete, and misleading information, surprise situations, and changes are to be expected.

IV-21

The general uncertainty inherent in all information creates a special problem. All decisions based on uncertain information take place in a kind of twilight, which obscures reality by an indeterminable amount. This obscurity tends to make things seem fantastic or threatening, perhaps larger or perhaps smaller than they really are. Whatever is hidden from full view in this feeble light must be guessed at by talent, or simply left to chance. This requires consideration and courage. But to think twice before taking action is quite sufficient for most situations.

IV-22

An executive cannot rely on the intelligence, ability, or hard work of his staff to produce success. Instead, he must furnish them with tasks which are capable of being completed. The art of leadership is an art based on simplicity; and all success is rooted in performance. There is nothing vague about this; everything is common sense. Successful leadership is the art of augmenting the chances which are in our favor by effective action. In leadership, it is important what one does. But it is also important how one does it. Strong determination and perseverance in carrying through simple ideas are the surest routes to one's objective.

IV-23

The art of leadership is like everything else that is uncomplicated and beautiful. The simplest moves are the best. Only what is simple can produce outstanding success. Hence, an effective executive solves problems by understanding the heart of a matter. An inferior executive, on the other hand, is likely to compound problems by seeing only superficial details.

IV-24

Simplicity contributes to successful actions. Complexity causes disorder, confusion, and failure. Direct, simple plans and clear, concise actions minimize disorder and confusion. If expected results are equal, the simplest method should always be preferred.

IV-25
Petty minds attempt to accomplish everything; wise men pursue only the most important. There is an ancient saying: He who would accomplish everything, accomplishes nothing. Therefore, always sacrifice the unimportant and pursue the essential! Major goals can only be achieved by decisive action. Therefore, the fundamental job of leadership consists of the following: Correctly determine how and when such decisive actions can be accomplished with the greatest probability of success.

V

Responsibility

Responsibility: A leader embraces the duties and obligations that grow from the trust and power given him. The most critical of these obligations are clear perception, determined action, and an overriding concern for the best interests of his constituents. A true leader owns up to the results of his decisions and actions and shares their consequences along with his constituents.

V-1
Leadership is not a prerogative, but rather a responsibility. Power and position are only given to enable you to better serve your constituents. They are not given for you to exercise your idiosyncrasies.

V-2

An effective leader has nine responsibilities to which he must constantly attend:

1. To see clearly when he looks
2. To hear correctly when he listens
3. To think carefully when he speaks
4. To inquire critically when he doubts
5. To show respect when he serves
6. To maintain calm when he is challenged
7. To consider consequences when he decides
8. To create desirable results when he works
9. To do what is right when he acts

V-3

The basics of responsible leadership are: Do not interfere in a subordinate's duties. If a person performs as expected, give him a free hand. If he hesitates, help him out. If he fails, change his responsibilities. But people whose performance is consistently poor should be trained carefully and supervised closely.

V-4

To develop his power to influence others, a leader practices doing these things: He creates respect and esprit de corps. He encourages trust and loyalty. He instills confidence and purpose.

V-5

An effective leader, while aware of his own abilities, does not become arrogant. He associates with those like him, but does not form cliques.

V-6

Within his own organization, a responsible leader is respectful to those above him and reserved with those beneath him. When dealing with outsiders, he is calm and assured but careful when he speaks. When working with lower-level employees, an effective leader is pleasant and efficient. When working with those higher in the organization, he is polite and unpretentious. When summoned by the highest managers, he is confident but formal.

V-7

Strength of personality counts for only so much. Manners and appearance command respect in the long run only when a leader is capable of carrying out his tasks. The criterion of leadership is the ability to think clearly and work hard rather than to look good.

V-8

Do not overly concern yourself with matters which are not your responsibility. Allow the other fellow to do his job without hindrance.

V-9

Do not do to others what you would not want them to do to you.

V-10

No matter how technically capable a leader may be, if he loses the trust of his constituents, he will inevitably fail.

V-11

Decisive leadership is critical to success, and nowhere is this more important than in higher-level executives. Executives who become depressed when things are not going well and who lack the drive to get things done, and the determination to see their plan through to the end, are useless. They are, in fact, worse than useless— they are a liability, since lack of drive and determination quickly affects employee morale.

V-12

By paying careful attention to small details of behavior, a leader can recognize both deception and weakness in other people. This is particularly important in situations where deception and weakness are not normally ex- pected—such as dealing with trusted advisors.

V-13

You cannot carve a piece of rotten wood into a beautiful statue, nor build a strong wall with bricks made of manure. Neither can you assign important responsibilities to an ignorant person.

V-14

Beware of clever and conspicuous people. They are seldom loyal. A perceptive leader does not believe someone solely because of his eloquence or reputation; on the other hand, neither does he reject otherwise useful information because of the character or appearance of the messenger.

V-15

An effective leader avoids certain kinds of people. He avoids those who criticize and gossip; those who envy success; those who are aggressive, but lack discipline; those who are intolerant and inflexible; those who steal or lie; those who are insubordinate and ill-mannered; and those who show poor judgment and weak spirit.

V-16

The greatest responsibility of a leader is to decide. Committees, meetings, discussion groups, and so forth are the enemies of vigorous and prompt action. Their danger increases geometrically with their number and size. Committees are mostly burdened with doubts and are concerned about petty problems. In the face of uncertainty, they inevitably adopt the worst course of action, which, under conditions of change, conflict, chaos, and uncertainty is always the most timid, or, if you will, the most prudent. This leaves you open to ambush, since your most prudent course is also the most obvious to your competitor.

V-17

Within your own organization, be careful about how you deal with small-minded people. If you become familiar with them, they are likely to be disrespectful. If you remain distant, they can turn sullen. Remember, too, that small-minded people are ambitious and allow their emotions to cloud their reason. They do not see clearly the consequences of their actions.

V-18

If you need help in fighting a battle, do not enlist someone who would grab a tiger by the tail or jump into a raging river without thinking about life or death. Instead, find someone who faces difficulties with a responsible attitude and who achieves his objectives by properly executing carefully considered plans.

V-19

A leader, above all, exhibits a cool head—that is, he objectively processes information and correctly estimates its impact on his situation. Two qualities must accompany coolness. The first is decisiveness. Without decisiveness, other qualities are of little value. The second is intelligence. The leader should have a talent for turning every situation into an advantage, for creating unexpected, but appropriate, improvisation in the face of obstacles. He should be able to fathom the intentions of other men, while keeping his own intentions to himself.

V-20
Do not speak out on an issue until it is straight in your mind. A defect in white jade can be polished away, but no amount of polish can erase a defective word. A team of fast horses cannot catch up with careless words once they are spoken.

V-21
During change and chaos, the leader's first responsibility is to grasp the actual situation, which is almost always hidden in a mist of uncertainty; that is, to assess the known elements correctly and to guess the unknown elements accurately. Then he must reach a decision quickly and carry it out forcefully and relentlessly.

V-22
A cardinal responsibility of a leader is to foresee where and when crises affecting his constituency are likely to occur. But even if a leader makes right decisions, events may not cooperate. Keep the possibility of unpreventable failure in your mind in order to deal with the consequences.

V-23
A leader who does not prepare for difficulties when they are distant will not escape them when they are close.

V-24

An effective leader does not propose a certain course of action until he has carefully looked at the difficulties and consequences involved. He studies how things will work before he speaks of them.

V-25

Take great care when everyone disagrees with you. But take even greater care when everyone agrees.

V-26

An effective leader respects the opinions of others, but thinks for himself and makes up his own mind. An ignorant person, on the other hand, does not think for himself; neither does he respect any opinion which differs from his own.

V-27

If a leader is tolerant, he will earn respect. If he is trustworthy, he will be given responsibility. If he is diligent, he will surpass expectations. If he is fair, he will not make enemies. Earn trust by performing your duties in a responsible manner. Do your best for those who employ you. Keep your promises to them. Refuse to associate with those who promote mediocrity. Recognize and correct your own faults.

V-28

A responsible leader can influence those with power in an organization, even at a distance; an ignorant person, on the other hand, can influence only those over whom he holds power, and even then, only when they are close by.

VI
Knowledge

Knowledge: The foundation of successful leadership. Knowledge has three aspects. The first, *fundamental knowledge*, deals with studying science, history, and human nature; in other words, learning the basics of the art of leadership. The second, *strategic knowledge*, concerns understanding the needs and goals of both constituents and competitors and planning effective operations to reach objectives. The third, *tactical knowledge*, focuses on uncovering evolving threats and opportunities and responding swiftly and appropriately to them, within the strategic framework, through innovation and improvisation.

VI-1
What is knowledge? To understand that you know something when you do, and to admit that you do not know something when you do not. That is knowledge.

VI-2
Seek understanding like a thirsty man lost in the desert seeks water—with fearful determination.

VI-3
True sophistication can only be attained by mixing natural talent with appropriate amounts of education, experience, and culture. Untrained people, even those with talent, are clumsy and likely to stumble.

VI-4
Learn by observing the behavior of other people. If you observe good behavior, copy it. If you observe bad behavior, look for the same behavior in yourself and eliminate it.

VI-5
A person who delights in the pursuit of knowledge and who does not hesitate to learn from others is truly on the path of excellence.

VI-6
A leader has no basis for judging other people unless he studies history. To compete in business without a thorough knowledge of history is on par with the carelessness of a doctor who prescribes medicine without taking time to understand the disease he is treating.

VI-7

In competition, most of the time, the indirect approach is preferable to the direct approach; that is, the unexpected is generally more effective than the expected. The art of using the indirect approach can only be mastered, and its full scope appreciated, by study of and reflection on the whole history of leadership—political, business, and military. One factor remains paramount in all situations: Success in the indirect approach depends entirely on the quality—timeliness, accuracy, sufficiency—of competitive information available.

VI-8

We can crystallize two principles for using direct and indirect approaches to competitive situations, one negative, the other positive. First, negative: No company is justified in directly challenging a competitor *who is firmly positioned in a market or constituency* without a clear knowledge of the competitor's vulnerability. Second, positive: For a direct challenge to succeed, a competitor's equilibrium must be upset, using indirect methods, before the challenge is launched.

VI-9

People who reject education, yet who are ignorant; people who oppose discipline, yet who are ambitious; people who lack experience, yet who are outspoken— do not depend on these fools.

VI-10

Some people claim to have inherited intuitive genius from their ancestors or their college professors. How fortunate for them! For those of us who have not, however, the only alternative is to listen carefully and observe closely. Knowledge and experience, combined with study and reflection, will have to substitute for our lack of genius.

VI-11

If you fail to teach someone who could benefit from the lesson, you waste a person. If you attempt to teach someone who cannot benefit from the lesson, you waste your time. A wise leader wastes neither people nor time.

VI-12

Putting employees to work without adequate training destroys effectiveness and squanders enthusiasm.

VI-13

In business, even in the largest companies, goods and services are provided by small groups of people. Place emphasis on small-group instruction so that communication, coordination, and morale within these groups remains high.

VI-14

Business failure starts with the small groups which provide goods and services to the customer. Company growth is determined by their success. Skillful senior executives can strategically invest resources into favorable market situations, but the small-group leaders at the customer-contact level are the ones who really earn the profit. In a competitive situation, given equal resources, the best-trained company will win. Even if the odds are against it, a company which has well-trained small groups and small-group leaders will often outperform seemingly superior competitors.

VI-15

The more a group lacks in actual competitive experience, the more it needs to make use of history for its instruction. Although history is no substitute for actual experience, it can be a solid foundation for quickly and effectively learning from that experience.

VI-16

The first quality of a leader is great knowledge. Knowledge does not come from intuition, but is the result of study and experience. A man is not born a leader. He must become one. Not to be anxious; to be always cool; to avoid confusion; to make appropriate decisions in the midst of confusion and chaos with as much composure as if he were perfectly at ease. These are proofs of knowledge.

VI-17

Just as a master craftsman perfects his skill by working long hours in his shop, an effective leader increases his knowledge by organized study and careful thought.

VI-18

A leader is truly innovative when he combines modern tools with proven wisdom to accomplish desirable results.

VI-19

A leader who studies widely to broaden his understanding, but acts within the bounds of tradition and common sense, is not likely to go far wrong.

VI-20

A leader can never act with confidence until he is master of his profession. The whole training of an executive should seek to accomplish one purpose—to instill in him the ability to lead the company in a time of change, conflict, chaos, and uncertainty.

VI-21

The ever-successful executive is rare, and there have been few of these in history. What is necessary is that executives should have studied the art of leadership and paid attention to its rules; it is then that, with this wisdom tempered by courage and technical skill, even ordinarily talented executives will increase the company's chances of success.

VI-22
A competent leader can get efficient service from poor employees, while, on the contrary, an inept executive can and will demoralize the best.

VI-23
While it is possible, through accident or birth, for an incompetent person to hold high rank in an organization, it is not possible for an incompetent person to be an effective leader. Promote only those who have proven themselves competent!

VI-24
The true way to be popular with employees is not to be free and familiar with them, but to make them believe you know more than they do and have their best interests at heart.

VI-25
Never despise your competitor, whoever he is. Try to find out about his methods of operation and means of accomplishing his goals, how he thinks and how he competes. Research his strengths and weaknesses. How can any executive say what he should do when he is ignorant of what his competition is up to?

VI-26

If you know a competitor's plans beforehand, you will always be more than a match for him, even with inferior resources. All executives who lead companies try to obtain this information. It is difficult to discern the competitor's real plans, and to detect the truth in all the reports and data one receives. To guess at the intention of a competitor; to understand his opinion of you; to hide your intentions and opinions from him; to mislead him by giving out incomplete or incorrect information; to deceive the competition and disguise your schemes, so as to always compete under the best conditions—this is the art of competitive leadership.

VI-27

The greatest executive is he who makes the fewest mistakes, and mistakes incubate inside closed minds. Preconceived notions, unchallenged assumptions, folk wisdom, and the like, especially under competitive conditions, are dangerous, because they give their own particular color to all information that comes in and stifle any real understanding of the actual situation.

VI-28

All executives must have freedom of mind, no prejudices, no prepossession, no fixed ideas. No opinion should be accepted without facts to support it. No course of action should be taken merely because it has always been taken before.

VI-29

The success of an executive during competition does not arise from following rules or models. It consists in obtaining an absolutely clear and accurate comprehension of the dominant facts of the situation at the time, along with all the forces at work. Every competitive operation is unique. What is required is a profound, objective appreciation of the actual events occurring now. There is no surer road to disaster than to fit past solutions, however successful, to current situations.

VI-30

An executive is wise to carefully study the actual situation, in order to take advantage of his strong points and reduce the impact of his weaknesses. There is no greater proof of an executive's talent than his ability to develop workable, productive strategies based on accurate and objective evaluation of information.

VI-31

When making a plan, try to put yourself into the minds of your constituents and competitors. Think what course of action is most likely to benefit your constituents; what course is least likely to be expected and countered by your competitors. The surest way to success is to choose the course of least expectation.

VI-32

He who does not carefully compare his own resources with those required for completion of a task will come to a disastrous end.

VI-33

An executive in all his projects should not think so much about what he wishes to do as what his competition will do. He should never underestimate the competition, but put himself in the competitor's place in order to understand the situation from that point of view. In this way, his plans will not be upset by unexpected events because he will have foreseen everything. An executive should think through all of the situations likely to occur around him. Who can attempt to accomplish what he does not understand? Who is able to furnish assistance in situations whose circumstances he does not understand?

VI-34

To be practical, any plan must take account of a competitor's power to obstruct it; the best chance of overcoming such obstruction is to have a plan that can be easily varied to fit the circumstances expected. A plan, like a tree, must have branches if it is to bear fruit. A plan with a single aim is apt to prove a barren pole.

VI-35

Long and careful deliberation, when followed by precise execution, promises great returns, whereas hasty and impetuous executives usually commit serious blunders.

VI-36

Without knowledge and preparation, superior man-power and resources do not create an advantage. A company which is inferior in resources, but is knowledgeable and prepared, can often defeat a superior competitor by improvisation and innovation.

VI-37

See things as they really are. Even though other people may call a certain object "a vase," if it does not look like a vase nor perform the functions of a vase, can it really be a vase?

VI-38

Normally, there is no ideal solution to competitive problems; every course of action has its advantages and disadvantages. One must select the course which seems to offer the greatest probability of advantage under the circumstances and then pursue it resolutely. Accept the consequences. Any compromise is bad.

VI-39
When making a decision, an effective leader considers all sides of an issue, facts and opinion, without bias. An ignorant person will consider only his bias, without regard to facts or knowledgeable advice to the contrary.

VI-40
There are four things an effective leader should always avoid: conjecture, bias, inflexibility, and conceit.

VI-41
The central task in leading competitive operations is maintaining flexibility, a task most difficult to perform well. It is particularly difficult to be flexible when resources are limited. To do so requires subjective ability—tolerance for ambiguity—of a very high order. To do so requires overcoming the confusion, obscurity, and uncertainty peculiar to competitive situations and discovering the order, clarity, and certainty in them; only thus can opportunities be realized.

VI-42
Naturally, in the course of a business operation, one would like to fulfill the initial plan . . . but this is almost never possible. Therefore, ensure that both plans and resources are flexible and adaptable to circumstances. Your plans should foresee and provide for a next step in case of success, failure, or partial success—which is the most common case. Your attitude and your organi-

zation structure should allow exploitation of opportunity or adaptation to changing conditions in the shortest possible time.

VI-43
Activity provides information and generates opportunity. A leader should execute his carefully drawn plans with as little delay as possible. Benefiting from unforeseen opportunity is what cures problems and makes fortunes. Learn to profit from the immediate circumstances.

VI-44
It is of the utmost importance to company executives to have a good knowledge of the marketplace and of their own and their competitors' positions in it. Winning is often not a question of whether the executives of one company or another are more highly educated, or which company's executives have greater experience, but which executives have the better grasp of marketplace reality. This is particularly true when a situation develops, as it often does, for which the outcome cannot be predicted. At this point the executives involved must have firsthand knowledge; reports received secondhand rarely give the information needed for effective decisions.

VII

Laddership

Laddership: A leader understands the special nature of the social and moral contract between leaders and their constituents. The leader is dependent upon his followers for his power and, to a large extent, his ability to produce results. Therefore, he must work cooperatively with them to reach agreed-upon objectives. But, at the same time, strong leadership is one of the more important factors, if not the only absolutely necessary one, in the success of those human activities that depend upon cooperation. Therefore, a leader is charged with the responsibility of imposing, through the exercise of appropriate power, whatever level of order and discipline is required to meet objectives. He does this in part by using a system of rewards and penalties that is perceived as fair and just by his constituents.

VII-1

When there is no one in control, no leader, nothing useful or distinguished or profitable can be accomplished. This is true of all aspects of life, and especially true where competitive business is concerned. In competitive business, leadership vision combined with cooperative action is the only way to produce favorable results.

VII-2

An essential element in understanding the nature of leadership is that a leader works with thinking, feeling people. These people are afraid of failure, and suffer from anxiety, jealousy, disease, and fatigue. Some are ambitious, some are not. Some are competent, others are dull. Some are cooperative and loyal, others insubordinate and superficial. In short, they carry within themselves a thousand and one differences. To make them perform as a team, it is not enough for a leader to decide what should be done and issue the orders for carrying out his intentions. He must also create a spirit of confidence in those under him.

VII-3

Confidence is the foundation of success in business: each person's belief in his own competence, and his trust in the competence of other members of his group.

VII-4

Senior executives who complain about the low morale of their employees evidently do not realize that employee morale is a mirror of confidence in their leadership. Confidence in leaders is an integral element of organizational spirit.

VII-5

Honor them with recognition, present them with meaningful rewards, and people willingly come to join you. Treat them courteously, inspire them with confidence, and people willingly work hard. Give them training, provide the best equipment so they are safe and effective, and people willingly meet objectives and deadlines. Lead them personally, and people will be effective. Record even small accomplishments, reward even a little merit, and people are encouraged to do their best.

VII-6

An effective leader, through proper organization of tasks and appropriate delegation of responsibility, achieves his own success by assuring the success of others.

VII-7

What is the best way to manage employees? Treat them with courtesy. Consider their needs. Promote those who are competent. Train those who lack skills. Assign work according to individual abilities and according to what is appropriate and customary for a particular job.

VII-8

A leader need not handle every detail with his own hand, for if he is in a tight place, he can call on others to do it for him. What he needs first of all is the capacity to judge the abilities of the people he uses.

VII-9

An executive with intelligence and perception will be able to put others to use effectively. People's talents differ, and to use a person without evaluating his fitness for a particular task just because one has taken a liking to him may bring about failure. A man should be put to use according to his training and temperament. When an executive puts people to use like the carpenter uses curved wood for the wheel and straight wood for the axle, all people have value.

VII-10

A policy of rewards and penalties means rewarding merit and penalizing failure. Rewarding merit promotes achievement. Penalizing failure discourages incompetence. It is imperative that rewards and penalties be fair and impartial. When merit is rewarded, competent employees know what they are striving for; when failure is penalized, incompetent employees know what to fear. Therefore, rewards should not be given arbitrarily, and penalties should not be handed out unjustly. If rewards

are given for no reason, those who have worked hard
will be resentful. If penalties are applied unjustly, people will turn bitter.

VII-11
Praise and blame are effective tools when used carefully. Pass out neither praise nor blame unless it is
warranted. Make sure a person has earned your notice,
good or bad, before giving it.

VII-12
Three factors determine whether employees have confidence in their superiors. This is of vital importance
because confidence in superiors is the source whence
effectiveness is born. First, the rules and procedures of
the workplace must be followed by all. Established
rules and procedures cannot be violated. Second, equipment, training, and surroundings must be suitable for
the task. Third, employees and equipment must not be
overworked or demoralized. The enthusiasm and morale of your employees cannot be depleted. If these factors are ignored, employees will not trust their
superiors. If superiors are ineffective, when an organization must compete, it will be defeated.

VII-13
Those who would be senior executives must have people around them with loyal hearts, keen eyes and long
ears, sharp claws and curved fangs. Without advice
from people loyal to them, executives walk in the dark,

not knowing where to step. Without information from people with keen eyes and long ears, they are as though blind and deaf, not knowing where to proceed. Without protection from people with sharp claws and curved fangs, they are like warriors in battle without armor; inevitably they will die. Therefore, good leaders always have intelligent and learned associates for their advisors, thoughtful and careful associates for their eyes and ears, brave and formidable associates for their claws and fangs.

VII-14

Behavior, particularly under the influence of unusual conditions, will certainly reveal a person's basic character. Observe behavior closely in order to understand character.

VII-15

If you discover the goals a person cherishes; if you examine the means he employs to achieve them; if you investigate the people with whom he associates; if you observe the places he feels comfortable, then you will understand his character. As a leader, getting the right person into the right place at the right time is the central issue of success.

VII-16

Good habits are excellent, but they should also be governed by common sense and moderation. A person who is too courteous can become tedious. A person who is too careful, fearful. A person who is too courageous, reckless. A person who is too disciplined, intolerant.

VII-17
If you use your sharp wit and quick tongue to control or humble others, you will often make enemies.

VII-18
It is a disgrace to influence others with insincere words, a pretentious manner, or unnecessary deference. It is also a disgrace to cover up anger or disapproval with false friendship.

VII-19
If a person demands excellence from himself but much less from other people, he will have few difficulties in dealing with them.

VII-20
If you want to encourage mutual respect and teamwork in the workplace, always be courteous and considerate of others. Accomplishing worthwhile goals becomes easier when people respect each other and work harmoniously in teams.

VII-21
A leader can be called truly skillful in human relations when he values other people's strong points even after learning about their faults. An outstanding leader quickly overlooks small faults, errors, or wrongs. As a

result, he has few enemies. Petty disagreements can disrupt team spirit, just as small irritations and minor impatience can destroy great projects.

VII-22

One notable characteristic of an effective leader is that he does not have time to criticize other people. Never tell people how to do things. Tell them your objectives, and they will surprise you with their ingenuity. Further, you must be willing to support the honest mistakes of your subordinates if you wish to develop initiative and experience. A large part of confidence which results from good leadership is related to the feeling of being supported. It is the fear of being isolated which undermines enthusiasm and morale.

VII-23

Respect other people. Do not have them do what you would not do.

VII-24

Only after he has gained the confidence of his employees does a new leader demand extra work from them. If he does otherwise, employees will consider themselves misused. Only after he has gained the confidence of his own superiors does a new leader offer advice against unwise decisions. If he does otherwise, the superiors may consider him insubordinate.

VII-25

An effective leader, even if he has not mastered the details of each function under his control, will nevertheless manage broad responsibilities well because he knows how to use people according to their abilities. An inferior person, while he may be an acknowledged expert in narrow functional details, cannot manage broad responsibilities because he does not know people. It may be, and often is, true that there is merit without rank, but there is seldom rank without some merit. But when good fortune provides us with an important position, without our being adequately prepared for it, it is almost impossible for us to maintain ourselves suitably in it and appear worthy of possessing it.

VII-26

An effective leader praises those who are competent, while helping those who are not. In this way he encourages the best from everyone. An effective leader develops strength and retards weakness in others. The inferior person does just the opposite.

VII-27

The personal competence of a single individual alone is not decisive, but rather the combined competence of all members of an organization. The latter rests on the good opinion and the confidence each individual member places in the unit to which he belongs. The least effective members of an organization, if banded together appropriately, have their power. Four highly competent people who do not know each other well may not even attempt to solve a serious problem for fear of failure. But four less competent people who know each other well and are sure of their mutual reliability and capabilities will work resolutely at a solution. Solidarity and confidence in the face of pressure cannot be improvised; they must be learned over time.

VII-28

Personal popularity, however desirable it may be to individuals, will not build an organization, nor develop a market, nor pay the bills. Popularity will not enable an organization to compete effectively nor keep it running efficiently. Discipline is not intended to kill character, enthusiasm, and initiative, but to develop them. The purpose of discipline is to bring about understanding and cooperation for the attainment of common objectives.

VII-29

In competitive business operations, discipline and order lead to profit. If rewards and penalties are unclear, if rules and regulations are unreliable, and if orders and directives are not followed, even if you have an organization with a million members and a billion dollars, these resources can be of no practical use.

VII-30
Employees always put the silence of their leaders in the worst possible light; they always assume no news is bad news, despite proverbs to the contrary. Fear demoralizes.

VII-31
The need for truth is not always realized. A leader must speak the truth to those under him; if he does not, when they find out, they will lose confidence in him.

VII-32
No matter how lacking a man may be in other respects, if he aspires to leadership, he should first of all tell no lies. It is basic that he is not the least bit suspicious and that he can always stand on his integrity. When a man who is known to have formerly told lies and acted suspiciously is placed in a position of power, neither his associates nor his competitors will believe in him, regardless of how reasonable his words may be. One should be very careful about this.

VII-33
The leader should have a good disposition free from arbitrariness, jealousy, bias, and hatred. He should punish failure without a qualm, but never punish from anger or unjustly. He should reward success quickly and often. He should administer rules with impartiality and objectivity. With these qualities, he will be feared by

some; he will be loved by others; but, without a doubt, he will be obeyed by all.

VII-34

Failure cannot be ignored, for nothing will reduce morale more quickly than lack of discipline. Morale, built on effective training and a system of fair rewards and just penalties, always fosters success.

VII-35

Employees who know that their leaders reward success and penalize failure are keener to be seen doing something right.

VII-36

What makes people under the stress of competition push ahead rather than retreat, even in the face of overwhelming odds, is the attitude and behavior of their leadership. When people know their leaders care for them, notice them, and reward their successes, they will attempt difficult tasks without hesitation. They do this as a reflection of the attitude of their leaders. In people's minds, nothing can replace the inspiration and lift that comes from a leader's noticing a job well done.

VII-37

Many people think that it is incorrect application of organizational behavior theories that creates strained relations between executives and employees. Strained relations are a matter of basic attitude, of executives and employees lacking mutual respect. The habit of talking down to employees is one of the worst vices that can afflict an executive. The value of tact cannot be overemphasized. Do not look down on others because you outrank them. Encourage and listen well to the words of your subordinates. It is well known that the most valuable minerals lie hidden in the ground.

VII-38
If you want people to work together well, to follow orders, to reach objectives, you must minimize form and maximize substance. First organize what is close, then organize what is far away. First organize what is inside, then organize what is outside. First organize what is easy, then organize what is difficult. First organize what is flexible, then organize what is brittle. First organize what is simple, then organize what is complex. First organize your own affairs, then organize those of others.

VIII
Example

Example: A leader's actions become a model for the actions of his constituent group. Further, the leader's character sets the moral tone of leadership. The standards he sets become the benchmark for the group. The people he favors become his flag-bearers. In all situations, the leader is observed and copied; at all times, the leader demonstrates preferred behavior by his own actions. The leader sets the example whether he intends to or not!

VIII-1
If an executive values competence in his own work, employees will value competence in theirs. The actions of executives are like the wind, while those of employees are like the grass. When the wind blows, the grass bends in the same direction.

VIII-2

It is proper for persons of great ability and high ambition to strive for wealth and power. But do not deceive yourself about these things! Wealth and power gained by forfeiting the principles underlying your character cannot possibly bring you contentment. Moreover, how can you claim to be an example for others to follow if you ignore your own principles—even if only for a little while? After all, a petty thief does exactly the same thing. Encourage people to strive for excellence by striving for excellence yourself. Lead by example!

VIII-3

In times of challenge, an effective leader is calm and confident; an inept person is tense and nervous. The spirit of success encourages the one, while the specter of failure haunts the other.

VIII-4

You cannot erase the past with words. Do not second-guess decisions that have already been made. Do not undermine actions already begun. Do not assign blame for errors already made. Rather, focus your attention on doing the best thing in the present moment.

VIII-5

How can you give the example of outstanding leadership? Do your best for those to whom you owe a duty. Put quality of service before reward. Strive for excellence. Show enthusiasm for routine tasks. Practice good manners. Consider others. When action is necessary, give all you have. Develop what is good in others; minimize what is bad. Help others to succeed by setting a standard of hard work and loyalty. Promote people who have talent; train those who lack skill.

VIII-6

An effective leader exhibits certain qualities: In relationships with his peers, he is polite and discreet. In serving his employers, he is diligent and respectful. In managing his employees, he is considerate and fair. In giving rewards to those who deserve them, he is generous. An effective leader is serious yet approachable, assertive yet courteous, determined yet relaxed.

VIII-7

If work rules are enforced by punishment, employees will avoid trouble by following the rules; punishment will not, however, motivate them to work harder. If, on the other hand, employees are guided by good example from above, treated with courtesy and trust, and encouraged by realistic expectations, they will not only strive to do better, but also gain a sense of personal pride and ownership in their work.

VIII-8

A superior executive is easy to work with, but difficult to satisfy because he will not be satisfied by anything less than excellence. But, when working with others, he assigns them tasks according to their abilities and does not demand more than they are capable of doing. An ignorant person, on the other hand, is easy to satisfy but difficult to work with. He will be satisfied as long as others cater to his opinions and biases. But, when working with others, he not only assigns them inappropriate tasks, but also demands perfection regardless of capability or experience.

VIII-9

Most of the time a person will not be able to please everyone. Since this is true, if you have a choice, it is probably better to please those who are competent and displease those who are not.

VIII-10

If an executive demonstrates effective leadership by practicing diligence, organization, and loyalty, his employees will perform their assigned tasks even without supervision. However, if a person displays arrogance and poor work habits himself, even close supervision of employees will not yield desirable results. A person who is diligent and loyal himself will have no difficulty influencing others to act the same.

VIII-11

When employees take the initiative and do not complain, this means they are motivated by the promise of success and do not fear failure. When an executive can get his employees to plunge right into the thick of a

EXAMPLE   101

crisis, it is his authority and example that brings this about.

VIII-12

The ability to lead people in difficult situations is a matter of using the authoritative power of the executive in charge. If an executive can wield his authority during a crisis by effectively focusing the combined power of his group, then he is able to attack problems like a fierce tiger with wings, flying over the four seas, going into action confidently whenever there is an opportunity. If an executive loses his authority and cannot focus the power of his group, he is like a dragon cast into a lake; he may seek the freedom of the high seas, but he is trapped and cannot get loose.

VIII-13

Character is the bedrock on which the whole edifice of leadership rests. With character, the full worth of the individual and his team can be realized. Without it, failure or, at best, mediocrity will result. Character is a habit. It is created through the daily choice of right and wrong. It is a moral quality which grows gradually to maturity. It does not appear suddenly.

VIII-14

Your organization is a reflection of yourself. By greatness of character, an executive gains command over himself. By consistency and competence, he gains the respect of his subordinates. The success of the entire group is based on the firmness of the conduct of the executive who will manage it.

VIII-15

One should not carry malice in his heart. If a malicious person is in a high position, his constituents will fight among themselves continuously. Civility is both rational and farsighted, for it endows the person who displays it with a sense of superiority and encourages cooperation among people.

VIII-16

What is the truest test of human character? It is probably this: that a person will know how to be patient in the midst of hard circumstance, and can continue to be personally effective while living through whatever discouragements beset him and his associates.

VIII-17

An executive should be professional in his attitudes, naturally suited for command, profound in his thinking, sound in his judgment, hardworking, and emotionally stable. He should instill respect in his subordinates through an appropriate system of rewards and penalties. He should be kind, gracious, and civil under most circumstances, but stern when necessary. Above all, an executive must be judged by his actions, and it is preferable that he be chosen for command on the basis of his example.

Example 103

VIII-18

If wise, an executive is able to recognize changing circumstances and to act expediently. If consistent, his subordinates will have no doubt of the certainty of rewards and punishments. If fair, he respects both his associates and subordinates, empathizes with the difficulties others may face, and appreciates their industry and toil. If courageous, he gains success by seizing opportunity without hesitation. If disciplined, his subordinates are encouraged by his example of competence and high moral tone.

VIII-19

Intelligence, knowledge, and experience are important prerequisites of executive success. But lack of these may, if necessary, be compensated for by a good staff. Strength of character and inner fortitude, however, are the decisive factors. The confidence of the employee group is based solely upon the executive's strength of character.

VIII-20

No matter what happens, it is the part of the executive in charge to remain firm and constant in his purposes; he must show neither excessive elation in prosperity, nor deep depression in adversity. In business, both good and bad results are expected and follow each other by turns. Employees usually estimate the probability of success or the consequences of failure by the demeanor of their chief executive.

VIII-21

In connection with managing difficult or challenging situations, one must never say that something absolutely can not be done. By saying this, the limitations one has set in one's mind will be exposed to his associates. An executive should never display a weak attitude if he expects to overcome difficult situations. If an executive loses his courage, his associates and subordinates will lose their respect for him. However desperate the situation, a senior executive must always exude confidence. Anxiety at the top spreads like cancer through the organization.

VIII-22

If an executive is in a hurry to finish some project that he has in process, he should not hesitate to pitch in and give his employees a hand. There is no greater encouragement to employees than the example of higher executives.

VIII-23

According to the code of effective leadership, executives do not say they are thirsty before the employees have drawn water from the well; executives do not say they are hungry before the employees' food is cooked; executives do not say they are cold before the employees' fires are lit. Executives do not use fans in summer,

EXAMPLE   105

do not wear leather in winter, do not use umbrellas in the rain. They do as everyone else does. Thus they earn both respect and power.

VIII-24
An executive should set an example of how things ought to be done, training himself to the highest standards of his profession, doing what is right and refraining from doing those things he himself has prohibited.

VIII-25
Essential to leadership is to share the rewards and problems of subordinates. If you encounter difficulties, do not abandon your group to save yourself, do not seek personal escape from the challenges confronting you. Rather, make every effort to protect your subordinates and associates, sharing their fate. If you do this, your constituents will not forget you. The executive who spends more late nights with his people and who works harder in training his subordinates runs the fewest risks of failure.

VIII-26
Be an example to your group, both in your professional activities and in your private life. When faced with fatigue or difficulties, never spare yourself at the expense of your subordinates. Even under the worst circumstances, always be tactful and well mannered.

VIII-27

Competitive business operations is a special kind of activity, different from the administrative and procedural aspects of organizations. An organization's success in competition depends on individuals who are steeped in the spirit and essence of competitive activity; who train for the demands of competition; who apply their intelligence to every detail; who gain competence and confidence through practice; and who completely immerse their personalities in winning.

VIII-28

In moments of chaos, fatigue, or disorganization, or when something out of the ordinary is required, the personal example of the leader works wonders, especially if he has had the foresight to create some sort of mystique around himself. One of the most valuable qualities of an executive is the flair for putting himself in the right place at the critical time. When the situation becomes critical, employees must see their executives and know them to be near. It does not matter even if the executives cannot do a great deal to change the circumstances. Their presence creates a belief that direction exists, and that is enough to maintain effort.

VIII-29

An executive skilled at leading competitive activities is like a person sitting in a leaking boat or lying under a burning roof. Under difficult circumstances, the leader

EXAMPLE 107

knows there is no time for the wise to offer advice nor for the brave to be angry. All must focus their efforts on the demands of the situation at hand. Therefore, it can be said that of all the dangers involved in leading competitive operations, timidity is the greatest. Most of the calamities which overtake an organization in competition arise from hesitation and fear of failure.

Section III

LESSONS IN LEADERSHIP

The SPARKLE Principles were developed with reference to the lives of real people. The following seven chapters provide discussions and examples of the attitudes and actions of people in leadership situations to illustrate and amplify the SPARKLE Principles. The leaders covered in these lessons are George Washington, Robert E. Lee, Winston S. Churchill, Ulysses S. Grant, Thomas A. Edison, George C. Marshall, T. E. Lawrence, and Dwight D. Eisenhower. I selected these individuals from the hundreds of examples available because they are generally familiar to most people and there are many authoritative sources available for each one.

IX

Self-Discipline

Self-Discipline: A leader tends to live by a set of rules or principles that he determines are appropriate for him and acceptable to his constituents. A leader does not need external motivation to ensure performance.

George Washington: Code of Conduct and Ethics

Every great leader goes through the process of self-determination. During this process, a leader determines what group he intends to lead and the rules and behaviors required by that group. A leader must decide to accept the rules and behaviors required, regardless of what anyone else thinks and, more importantly, regardless of the consequences. The leader must act in a manner which is consistent with the required rules and behaviors. But do not delude yourself. A real leader "walks the walk," or he cannot really lead.

The often-told story of young George Washington and the cherry tree is, of course, a myth. But, as with many myths, the essential truth behind the story is not. As a young man, General Washington organized and wrote out, as a school exercise, one hundred ten "Rules of Civility and Decent Behavior in Company and Conversation." These rules formed the basis of his code of conduct and ethics in adult life and created an unshakable foundation for his eventual rise to power and leadership.

George Washington was not an intellectual giant; he was not well educated when compared to some of the other men involved in the Revolutionary War. He was a great military leader in the sense that his overall strategy worked (that is, he correctly assessed the strengths of his army and the weaknesses of the British army in America and exploited both), not because of brilliant battlefield execution. Washington's plans were almost always too complicated for his army to carry out. They worked at times because of good fortune, but generally not in the way he intended. A good example of this is his attack across the Delaware River. It succeeded magnificently because he caught the enemy completely unprepared, not because his forces arrived at the correct place on time. Nevertheless, at the end of the Revolutionary War, Washington was the most revered and trusted leader in America. His followers trusted him because he did not set himself above or outside the ideals of the revolution for which he fought. He could have become king of the United States; but he scorned the very thought of such a misuse of power because it violated his code of self-discipline. Throughout his life, he acted according to his understanding of the requirements of the confidence given him by his constituents— a confidence based on his strict adherence to a code of conduct and ethics.

Here are but a few examples drawn from Washington's "Rules of Civility . . .":

- When you speak, be short and comprehensive.
- Do not argue with your superior; submit your ideas to him modestly.
- When a subordinate does his best, even if he does not succeed, do not blame him.
- When you must give advice or criticism, consider whether it should be given in public or private; whether it should be given now or at some other time; and in what manner it should be given. If you must criticize someone, do so carefully.
- If you are admonished by your superior, do not argue at the time. Rather, if you are not at fault, tell your superior the facts later.
- Do not make fun of anything important to others.
- If you criticize others for some fault, make sure you eliminate it from yourself first. A good example speaks much louder than words.

- Do not be in haste to believe bad reports about others.
- Associate yourself with other good people; it is better to be alone than in bad company. Do not speak about others with malice or envy.
- Always allow reason to govern your actions.
- Never break the rules in front of your subordinates.
- A man should not overly value his own accomplishments.
- Do not detract from others, nor be overbearing when giving commands.
- Do not speak badly of those who are not present.
- Do not go where you are not wanted.
- Do not give unasked-for advice.
- If your subordinates disagree, do not take one side or the other. Keep your opinion flexible. With unimportant matters, stay on the side of the majority.
- Make no comparisons among people.
- Do not be quick to talk about something if you do not know it is true.
- Some matters are better kept a secret. Do not be curious about the affairs of others.
- Do not start what you cannot finish.
- Keep your promises.

These rules could easily have been written by Sun Tzu and Confucius.

George C. Marshall: Clarity and Commitment

Study widely; inquire sincerely; adhere steadfastly to your principles; consider carefully your experiences, what works and what does not work for you. It is in doing these things that you will discover the meaning of excellence. Moreover, find the best leaders and copy their methods. In this way, you will also discover the meaning of leadership. There is no reason to follow someone who talks about leadership but is unwilling to pay the price for it. Excellence in leadership or anything else is not something remote or even difficult to find. We need only practice self-discipline, and it will begin to appear in our lives!

During World War II, the most important general in the U.S. Army never led an army into battle. Yet his decisions were critical to the success of the war effort. In 1939, General George Marshall was selected by President Franklin Roosevelt over a number of more senior generals to become the Army's Chief of Staff, the highest-ranking officer in the U.S. military. At this time, the U.S. army's active duty roster ranked twentieth in the world, just one place ahead of Bulgaria.

Under Marshall's command the Army grew from a poorly trained and badly equipped force of 174,000 men to a staggering 8.3 million superbly trained and supplied soldiers. How did he accomplish this feat? He did it by clearly understanding the task at hand and by committing himself to the success of the war effort, setting aside his ego when necessary to benefit the cause.

General Marshall served on the staff of General Pershing with the American Expeditionary Force in France during World War I. At the end of the war, Marshall had some very definite ideas about how the Army needed to be improved if it were to effectively fight the next war. In 1927, Marshall was named assistant commandant in charge of the curriculum of the Infantry School at Fort Benning, Georgia, and for the next few years worked to change the Army's methods for training infantry officers. Marshall's field exercises highlighted the uncertainty of battlefield situations and the scarcity and unreliability of information. He emphasized the need for timely, effective decisions under stress. He said: "We must remove the complications and difficulties [in giving orders]. We must concentrate on certain vital considerations . . . methods so simple that officers with good common sense can readily grasp the idea." (In other words, do the essential things well!) His influence on the Army was pervasive. Over two hundred future generals attended or taught at the Infantry School during his tenure there.

Marshall clearly understood the kind of person required to lead troops during wartime. Lack of leadership ability or lack of physical capacity would cost American lives. Marshall stated his philosophy for weeding out incompetent or unsuitable officers: "I'm going to put these men to the severest tests which I can devise. I'm going to shift them into jobs of greater responsibility than those they hold now. Then I'm going to change them suddenly, without warning, to jobs even more burdensome and difficult . . . I'm going to let them think I am treating them arbitrarily and asking too much from them. Those who stand up under the punishment will be pushed ahead. Those who fail are out at the first sign of faltering." Virtually every general officer serving in the U.S. Army in 1939 had to be replaced by 1944.

Eric Larrabee describes Marshall's leadership style in his book *Commander in Chief*: "Marshall liked having men around him who were willing to make decisions without waiting to be told what to do; they were not only permitted but expected to contradict him when they disagreed. He did not want to have presentations from anyone who was not prepared to recommend a line of action and defend it. He tired of inarticulate briefing from his staff officers and told them to find 'three or four bright young men who can talk' and have them condense the subjects he needed into ten-minute summations . . ."

The most prestigious position of World War II was command of the invasion of France, Operation Overlord, in June 1944. The person leading the Allied force would become one of the most celebrated commanders in world history. Marshall was clearly the best qualified person to lead the invasion. Almost everyone believed that he should be accorded the honor. Marshall's future place in history would be guaranteed if he were commander. The trouble was that Marshall was too valuable as Chief of Staff. Naming him commander of Overlord would place him under the command of the next Chief of Staff (probably Eisenhower), creating an awkward command situation. Marshall was the only Army general who had the complete confidence of President Roosevelt and therefore had the power and authority to manage the war from Washington. President Roosevelt chose General Eisenhower for the command because, as he said to Marshall, "I don't feel that I could sleep at ease with you out of Washington."

It was typical of Marshall's self-disciplined character that he never told the President he wanted the command of Overlord. Eric Larrabee comments: "Marshall, in refusing to tell the President that he wanted the Overlord command, acted out of a noble effacement of self and self-interest. If self-denial can be said to increase the magnetic properties of a noble spirit, it did so in the case of General Marshall. The near total backing of the President, the unmatched esteem in which he was held by Congress, and the dominion he came to exercise over the Combined Chiefs (i.e., the heads of the Navy, Air Force, and Marine Corps)—all conspired to make Marshall a towering figure . . ."

X

Purpose

Purpose: A leader develops intense determination to achieve his vision and his objectives. Intense determination creates high morale and spirit among constituents. This allows the leader to effectively employ both personal and organizational power to accomplish goals. The leader uses this power to direct and control the efforts of his followers.

Ulysses S. Grant: Confidence in Crisis

Employees invariably reflect the attitude of their executive. The leader sets the tone. His spirit and his ability are naturally communicated to those who follow. There is an ancient saying: If you want to win a battle, it is better to have an army of asses commanded by a lion than an army of lions commanded by an ass.

Leaders must deal with chaotic situations when their organizations are faced with uncertainty, change, and competition. Under difficult and trying circumstances, constituents depend on their leaders for confidence and order. Successful leaders become the eye of the storm, a calm, assuring reference point from which effective action can be undertaken. The military career of General Ulysses S. Grant gives two excellent examples of the power of calm confidence during a crisis.

Fort Donelson, located on the banks of Kentucky's Tennessee River, was a Confederate stronghold, defended by approximately 18,000 soldiers. In early 1862, Grant advanced on the fort with 15,000 men and a flotilla of gunboats and surrounded it. On the morning of February 15, 1862, Confederate forces launched an attack from the fort in an attempt to break Grant's lines, catching the Union troops off guard and Grant, a few miles away, discussing strategy with his flotilla commander.

The Confederate attack caused great confusion in the Union lines, driving a large portion of the men back. When Grant arrived, he met a staff officer, "white with fear," who told him that his army had been scattered. General Lew Wallace described the scene: "His face flushed slightly. With a sudden grip, he crushed the papers in his hand. But in an instant these signs of disappointment or hesitation cleared away. In his ordinary voice he said: ' . . . Gentlemen, the position on the right must be retaken.' With that he turned and galloped off."

Grant continued the story in his *Memoirs*: "I turned to Colonel J.D. Webster of my staff and said: 'Some of our men are pretty badly demoralized, but the enemy must be more so, for he has attempted to force his way out, but has fallen back; the one who attacks first now will be victorious and the enemy must be in a hurry if he [intends to] get ahead of me.' I determined to make the assault at once. It was clear to me that if our attack were to be made before the enemy could redistribute his forces, we would find little opposition. I directed Colonel Webster to call out to the men as we passed: 'Fill your cartridge boxes, quick, and get into line; the enemy is trying to escape and he must not be permitted to do so.' This acted like a charm. The men only wanted someone to give them a command." The attempted escape from Fort Donelson failed. The next day the fort surrendered. Grant's calm confidence rallied his men in the crisis.

A second example of Grant's leadership occurred during the Battle of Shiloh. On April 6, 1862, a Confederate army of some 40,000 men attacked Grant's army of about 40,000 men at Shiloh Meeting House in Tennessee. Grant was again away from the scene when the initial attacks occurred. At first the Confederates were completely successful, driving the Union forces back and overrunning several units. Grant returned at about 6 a.m. on the morning of the attack.

Major General J.F.C. Fuller, in his book *Grant and Lee: A Study in Personality and Generalship*, analyzes Grant's actions: "It was a spectacle of complete defeat, and any ordinary general would have planned a retreat, hoping to save some small fraction of his shattered army. But Grant was no ordinary general; for he was one of those rare and strange men who are fortified by disaster in the place of being depressed. He at once sent forward ammunition, organized reserves and then rode to the front. Between 6 a.m. and nightfall, he carried out eighteen important operations, stabilizing his shattered divisions [until reinforcements arrived]." The next day, Grant attacked, driving the Confederate army into retreat. Once again his calm confidence turned certain defeat into success. General Fuller continues: "Because of his dauntless spirit of resolution, far more so than through his genius, he had pulled his army out of the bogs . . ."

Winston S. Churchill: Uncommon Vision

Purpose is the motivating force for achievement. When you are doing something which serves your purpose, you are at your best. A man cannot use what he learns without the fire of purpose in his heart. The driving ambition of sincere purpose alone enables him to perform great accomplishments. Strength of purpose and self-discipline are decisive factors in the competitive marketplace. The confidence of the people around him is based upon an executive's strength of purpose. A leader should have a deep understanding of human nature and develop the ability to smooth out differences of opinion. He should have the power to gain affection while at the same time communicating urgency. He should possess the capacity for determined action at all times, and ruthless dedication when it is necessary. He needs to generate intense energy, but always keep a cool head. Purpose creates a determined state of mind. Determination results in steadfastness and courage and faith. It creates confidence and zeal and loyalty. It assures staying power and the will to win. An organization without purpose is nothing. With it, all things become possible.

All organizations must periodically evolve and change in order to overcome threats and take advantage of opportunities. The kind of leadership required for successful change and evolution is different from that required during less challenging times. Vision, strength of purpose, commitment, and determination must be communicated strongly and clearly to organization members in order to maintain the level of morale needed to survive and prosper during the inevitable uncertainty and conflict experienced during periods of organizational change. An outstanding example of leadership in crisis is provided by Winston Churchill during the early days of World War II.

Winston Churchill's public life was filled with controversy. He took firm stands that were often at odds with his political party's leadership. In November 1931, Churchill found himself outside the circle of influence because of his opposition to the independence of India. He still retained a seat in Parliament, but he had been removed from his place in the British cabinet. He was fifty-seven years old and feared that his dream of becoming Prime Minister of Britain was no longer attainable.

From 1931 until 1940, when he finally did become Prime Minister, he often spoke in Parliament about the growing threat from Nazi Germany. In February 1934, he said: "Wars come suddenly. I have lived through a period when one looked forward, as we do now, with anxiety and uncertainty to what would happen in the future. Suddenly something did happen—tremendous, swift, overpowering, irresistible . . . Not one of the lessons of the past has been learned, not one of them applied, and the situation is incomparably worse."

In November 1936, Churchill once again reminded the government (of which he was still not a part) of the danger: "Owing to past neglect, in the face of the plainest warnings, we have now entered upon a period of danger greater than has befallen Britain since the U-boat campaign was crushed; perhaps, indeed it is a more grievous period than that . . . The era of procrastination, of half measures, of soothing and baffling expedients, of delays is coming to a close. In its place we are entering a period of consequences . . . We cannot avoid this period; we are in it now."

In October 1938, when Prime Minister Neville Chamberlain brought Adolf Hitler's assurances from Munich that Europe would have "peace in our time,"

an alarmed Churchill declared: "I will begin by saying
the most unpopular and unwelcome thing. I will begin
by saying what everyone would like to ignore or forget
but which must nevertheless be stated, namely, that we
have sustained a total and unmitigated defeat . . . The
utmost the Prime Minister has been able to secure by
all his immense exertions, by all his great efforts, and
by all the anguish and strain through which we have
passed, the utmost he has been able to gain in the matters which were in dispute has been that the German
dictator, instead of snatching the victuals from the ta-
ble, has been content to have them served to him
course by course."

After the German army invaded Poland in Septem-
ber 1939, and then turned on France, the government
of Neville Chamberlain failed. Winston Churchill was
asked to form a new government, a government for wartime. The situation was bad. Everyone knew it. People
were afraid for their country and for themselves. Churchill's words to Parliament reflected an attitude of aggressive optimism and rallied the country behind his
vision of victory: "I would say to the House, as I have
said to those who have joined the Government: 'I have
nothing to offer but blood, toil, tears, and sweat.' We
have before us an ordeal of the most grievous kind. We
have before us many, many long months of struggle and
of suffering. You ask, What is our policy? I will say: It
is to wage war, by sea, by land and air, with all our
might and with all the strength God can give us . . . You
ask, What is our aim? I can answer that in one word:

Victory—victory at all costs, victory in spite of all terror, victory, however long and hard the road may be; for without victory, there is no survival."

Arguably, Churchill's greatest speech was given to the House of Commons after the evacuation of Dunkirk and the fall of France in June 1940. Another member of Parliament thought the speech "worth a thousand guns and the speeches of a thousand years." A deeply moved Churchill said: "I have, myself, full confidence that if all do their duty, if nothing is neglected, and if the best arrangements are made, we shall prove ourselves once again able to defend our island home, to ride out the storm of war, and to outlive the menace of tyranny, if necessary for years, if necessary alone . . . We shall not flag or fail. We shall go on to the end; we shall fight in France; we shall fight on the seas and oceans; we shall fight with growing confidence and growing strength in the air; we shall defend our island, whatever the cost may be; we shall fight on the beaches; we shall fight on the landing grounds; we shall fight in the fields and in the streets; we shall fight in the hills; we will never surrender . . ."

Imagine for a moment the uplifting impact of these positive words of defiance on the minds and emotions of the British people during that time of crisis. Victory in war cannot be won by vision alone; neither can profits in business. But vision, when sincerely communicated by a leader, can motivate the spirits of men and women, and that is the real key to winning wars and earning profits!

XI
Accomplishment

Accomplishment: A leader defines results in terms of meeting the needs of his constituents. Successful results are the foundation of leadership. Taking effective action is the basis for successful results. The elements of effective action are decision, determination, energy, simplicity, balance, and chance.

Robert E. Lee: Principles of Strategy

Success is gained only with vigor, decision, and unshaken determination; one must not grope or hesitate. The real leader displays his quality by winning over adversity, however great it may be. Action has three stages: (1) a decision to act based on analysis of the situation; (2) planning and preparation for action; and (3) the action itself. All three stages are

*influenced by the leader's determination. The ability
to act is rooted in determination, and for an effective
leader, determination is more important than intellect. Intellect without determination is ineffective;
but determination without intellect can be dangerous. There is always the danger of loss in competitive
activity, but we must decide between the possible loss
of inaction and the rewards and risks of action. The
essential thing is understanding the necessity to act
at the right time. Planning must be followed by effective execution. Execution is a matter of energy and
initiative. What an executive needs most is a balanced combination of practical intellect and energy.
Whatever is planned must be carried through. The
executive should understand that just as much energy is required of him as mental ability. Sensational success is, more often than not, a triumph of
energy rather than of intellect.*

General Robert E. Lee, commander of the Confederate
forces in Northern Virginia during the American Civil
War, is considered one of history's greatest leaders. His
army was outnumbered, outgunned, and undersupplied
for the entire four-year period it existed. Yet Lee's
forces fought the Union army to a standstill for three
years and, by remaining a continuous and viable threat
to the safety of Washington, D.C., gave the Confederate
States a real opportunity to win independence up until
the last year of the war. The strategy used by Lee to

achieve success in spite of all odds against him can be summed up in four principles:

1. High morale
2. Accurate and timely information
3. Opportunity and surprise
4. Effective execution

1. *High morale*. The Army of Northern Virginia, as Lee's forces were called, was composed of men who believed they were fighting for their political and personal freedom. They were highly motivated on an individual level, particularly at the beginning of the war. Lee was able to maintain their fighting spirit for several years, even through periods of great physical hardship and defeat. He did this through a combination of four factors. First, Lee himself believed in the correctness of his cause. He believed he was right and communicated this belief to his men through unshakable confidence and determined action. Second, Lee treated his men fairly and justly. He encouraged them to try to succeed. When they failed, he considered their individual personalities, aims, and the situation they found themselves in. When people succeeded, he gave them full credit. As a result, his men were not afraid to take the initiative. Third, Lee did not sacrifice his men unnecessarily, nor did he ignore their physical needs. When he asked them to attack, they knew an attack was required. Whenever food was available, Lee gave the best

of it to his men. Lee's staff fared no better in the field than did his soldiers. Lee managed his army's physical capacity carefully. He knew he could ask them to fight hard for four days, but on the fifth day they needed to rest. He made sure that the rest was available. Fourth, and perhaps most important, Lee won battles. The men were convinced that Lee knew how to win; and winning was, and is, the best way for soldiers to survive.

2. *Accurate and timely information*. Lee developed a network of spies and informants throughout Virginia. He knew exactly where the Union Army was, and whenever they moved he found out about it immediately. Thus he was always able to take advantage of the Union Army's weaknesses. Timely, accurate information made up for lack of troops and supplies.

3. *Opportunity and surprise*. Lee's victories were based on seeing opportunity and surprising the enemy. In the history of warfare, victory generally belongs to the larger, better supplied, and better equipped army, unless other strategic factors offset these advantages. Lee's was never the larger, better supplied, or better equipped army. He made up for these deficiencies by surprising the Union Army through rapid, unexpected movements. This type of strategy requires great self-control, great patience. Lee never underestimated his adversaries. He assumed their plans were sound and would work if no unforeseen event or mistake occurred. But Lee knew that unforeseen events and mistakes in execution were inevitable in battle. He would patiently wait until chance or error gave him a strategic advantage. Then he would quickly exploit his advantage. By

doing this, he was able to turn seemingly impossible situations into decisive victories.

4. *Effective execution.* Lee paid close attention to the temperaments and abilities of his men. In tough situations, it is necessary for a leader to match the requirements of the job to the temperaments and abilities of the people expected to accomplish the job. Some tasks are better suited to offensive-minded officers, some to defensive-minded ones. If the situation is critical, the temperament of the individual in command can greatly influence the outcome of events. Lee always sought to position people and units where they would do the most good. He had an intimate feel for the stamina and effectiveness of his men on both attack and defense. He knew their weapons. He knew their strengths and weaknesses. By maximizing their strengths and minimizing their weaknesses, he was able to effectively execute daring plans with the fewest possible men and smallest waste of ammunition and equipment.

It is interesting to note that when Lee had the opportunity to follow his own principles to the letter, he always won. Two battles—Chancellorsville and Fredericksburg—were resounding Confederate victories because Lee had the ability to plan and execute strategies that made the best use of the Confederate Army's strengths. Not surprisingly, Lee's greatest failure—Gettysburg—occurred when Lee could not (or did not, depending on whose version of the battle you read) follow his own strategic principles. At Gettysburg, his army still had high morale, but it lacked information, opportunity, surprise, and execution.

George Washington: Unexpected Tactics

No real success is possible unless an organization's executives are energetic, eager for responsibilities, and decisive; unless they can impart the will to see things through to profitable completion; and unless they are capable of exercising determination, good judgment, and control of emotion under pressure. Bold decisions give the best promise of success. But one must differentiate between a bold decision and a pure gamble. The outcome of a bold decision may not be success, but failure leaves one with sufficient resources to cope with whatever situation may arise. A pure gamble, on the other hand, is a decision which can lead either to complete success or to complete failure. Even a gamble may (and sometimes must) be justified, however, but only when circumstances leave no other choice. Success is composed of nothing more than taking advantage of accidents, and, although holding to sound management principles, an executive should never lose the opportunity to profit from one of these accidents; that is the mark of genius. In competitive business situations, there is always at least one favorable moment; the great skill is to recognize it and to seize it.

Every leader eventually must face the test of performance. Meeting the needs of constituents, particularly those needs that they cannot meet without the leader's ability, is the bottom line of leadership performance. As commander in chief of the Continental Army, George Washington was given by Congress the responsibility for creating a winning strategy and then executing that strategy through effective tactics. At the time of the American revolution, England was the most powerful nation on Earth, with virtually unlimited resources compared to those of the thirteen colonies. Washington was both outgunned and outmanned. His army was composed of frontiersmen, farmers, tradesmen, and soldiers of fortune, while the British had access to trained, professional soldiers. Even though many of his advisors wanted to wage a highly aggressive war, Washington knew the Continental Army could not go up against the British army and win. But, on the other hand, if Washington failed to maintain the momentum of the revolution by winning some kind of victory, he would be replaced. (There were plenty of other "patriot" generals available who thought they could run the army as well as or better than Washington.) Regardless of risk or difficulty, Washington needed to create a sense of confidence in the army's ability to win the war. Bottom-line accomplishment was required.

Things did not look promising for a successful action in December 1776. The battles fought in the summer and fall of 1776, the second year of the war, were disastrous for Washington. Although the British army could not destroy the Continental Army, in the battles that did occur, the Continentals led by Washington were beaten badly. The army's morale was extremely low. With enlistments for a great proportion of his army running out on January 1, 1777, Washington had every reason to be concerned. If he chose to delay action until spring arrived, he realized he might very well lose his position as commander in chief and possibly lose the war, too. Instead, Washington decided to try something unexpected.

The British army in New Jersey had been garrisoned at various points throughout the state to maintain control of the population. One of these garrisons, two to three thousand Hessian mercenary soldiers—supposedly the best troops money could buy—was at Trenton. Washington, drawing on his experience with successful Indian tactics in the French and Indian War, decided to execute a quick raid on the Trenton garrison. The plan called for crossing the Delaware River and marching nine miles to Trenton on Christmas Day 1776 to catch the Hessians by surprise. Even though the weather was miserable, the plan worked. The surprise was complete. Over nine hundred Hessians were captured. Not one American life was lost. The Continental victory over the cream of European mercenary troops sent shock waves throughout the world. For the first time, both Americans and Europeans could believe that Washington's army might actually win. The uplift in morale was immense and immediate.

A little more than a week later, Washington found himself trapped by a British force led by Lord Cornwallis, who wanted to quickly revenge the loss at Trenton and regain the momentum. Washington's troops were caught between an uncrossable river and the British soldiers. The British decided to rest their troops for the night and attack the trapped Continentals in the morning. This was standard procedure for a European army. Unfortunately for the British, the Continentals slipped away in small groups during the night and left only a few men to tend the campfires, giving the appearance that the army was still there.

But Washington did not retreat with his army. Instead he regrouped behind Cornwallis's force, destroyed British troops and captured supplies left at Princeton, and continued up the New Jersey peninsula into a strong defensive position at Morristown.

The British were astonished at this maneuver, because it would have been impossible for the British army to move so quickly and silently at night. Further, the British would never attempt to maneuver without an established supply line. As a result of this maneuver, the British were forced to retreat into New York City and give up New Jersey.

These two victories, won at great risk, were accomplishments that served as the foundation for ultimate victory in the Revolutionary War. They gave people confidence in their army. Washington's position as leader was solidified, and although Valley Forge and other political and military difficulties were still ahead of him, he was now confident that his army could survive and win in battle.

XII
Responsibility

Responsibility: A leader embraces the duties and obligations that grow from the trust and power given him. The most critical of these obligations are clear perception, determined action, and an overriding concern for the best interests of his constituents. A true leader owns up to the results of his decisions and actions and shares their consequences along with his constituents.

Lawrence of Arabia: Making the Hard Choices

Do not do to others what you would not want them to do to you. No matter how technically capable a leader may be, if he loses the trust of his constituents, he will inevitably fail. Decisive leadership is critical to success, and nowhere is this more important than in higher-level executives. Executives who become depressed when things are not going well and who lack the drive to get things done, and the determination to see their plan through to the end, are useless. They are, in fact, worse than useless—they are a liability, since lack of drive and determination quickly affects employee morale. A leader, above all, exhibits a cool head—that is, he objectively processes information and correctly estimates its impact on his situation. Two qualities must accompany coolness. The first is decisiveness. Without decisiveness, other qualities are of little value. The second is intelligence. The leader should have a talent for turning every situation into an advantage, for creating unexpected, but appropriate, improvisation in the face of obstacles. He should be able to fathom the intentions of other men, while keeping his own intentions to himself.

A leader is often called upon to make hard choices for his constituents. Further, the responsibilities of leadership may require the leader to carry out his decisions, regardless of personal risk or emotional consequences. Two episodes from the activities of Lieutenant Colonel T. E. Lawrence (Lawrence of Arabia) while fighting a guerrilla war with the Arab army against the Turks during World War I illustrate this aspect of leadership and responsibility. (Author's note: The immensely popular movie *Lawrence of Arabia*, made in the mid-1960s, accurately captures the essence of, and perhaps the emotions generated by, Lawrence's adventures during that period. The movie is, however, historically imprecise. The episodes described below are depicted in the movie, but not as they happened in real life. My sources for these accounts are Lawrence's own descriptions.)

During the war, it was necessary at times to form raiding parties and other groups made up of members from more than one Arab tribe. In those days, it was common for different tribes to be engaged in "blood feuds"; in other words, members of the same army were often tribal enemies. On one such trip, a quarrel between two men based on a blood feud ended in violence. One man shot and killed the other. The Arabs with Lawrence demanded that justice—in this case, execution of the man who did the shooting—be carried out immediately. The only problem was that any execution carried out by any Arab on any other outside his tribe would result in another blood feud, which would tear apart the group and endanger the mission. The only person who could execute the man was Lawrence himself because he was a foreigner and kinless, thus considered outside the realm of Arab tribal retribution.

Lawrence wrote: "Then rose up [in me] the horror which would make civilized man shun justice like a plague if he had not the needy to serve him as hangman for wages. I told Hamed [the guilty Arab] that he must die for punishment, and laid the burden for killing him on myself. At least no revenge could lie against my followers; for I was a stranger and kinless."

Lawrence did carry out the execution. The emotional consequences were devastating. He continued: "Afterwards the wakeful night dragged over me, until hours before dawn, I had the men [get] up and made them load. They had to lift me into the saddle."

Another event occurred during the march to attack Akaba, a seaport located at the north end of the Red Sea, on the east side of the Sinai peninsula opposite the Suez Canal. The Turks had fortified Akaba with large guns pointed out to sea, because the Turks believed the only way that Akaba could be attacked was from the sea. It was important for the British to control Akaba before invading Palestine because it would be needed as a supply point. Further, if left in Turkish hands, it would be in the rear of the British army and, as a result, would constitute a major threat. The British considered attacking Akaba by a landing from the sea, but had rejected the idea because it would have resulted in too many casualties and its success was doubtful. Lawrence's Arab forces could, however, successfully attack Akaba from the land side, particularly if the attack was a surprise.

On the march to Akaba, one of Lawrence's followers, Gasim, fell off his camel and was accidentally left behind while the group was crossing a particularly nasty stretch of the Nefud Desert in northwest Arabia. None of the other Arabs would risk their lives for "an ill-natured stranger, no charge to any of them . . ." Lawrence explained further: "That shifted the difficulty to my shoulders. Gasim was my man: and upon me lay the responsibility for him. I looked weakly at my trudging men, and wondered for a moment if I could send one of them back to the rescue. My shirking my duty would be understood because I was a foreigner: but that was precisely the [reason] I dare not do it. It would be impossible for me to influence the Arabs if I did not live by their rules. So, without saying anything, I turned my unwilling camel round, and forced her, grunting and moaning, into the emptiness behind. My temper was very unheroic, for I was furious with Gasim, a gap-toothed, grumbling fellow, bad-tempered, suspicious, and brutal. It seemed absurd that I should peril my weight in the Arab adventure for a single worthless man . . ."

Lawrence eventually rescued Gasim and thereby maintained the respect of the Arabs and their leaders. A few days later, Akaba was successfully taken, with almost no casualties, by fewer than six hundred Arabs on camels and horses from the land side, where the Turks did not expect them.

Dwight D. Eisenhower: Winning Ways

Leadership is not a prerogative, but rather a responsibility. Power and position are only given to enable you to better serve your constituents. They are not given for you to exercise your idiosyncrasies. To develop his power to influence others, a leader practices doing these things: He creates respect and esprit

*de corps. He encourages trust and loyalty. He instills
confidence and purpose. An effective leader, while
aware of his own abilities, does not become arrogant.
Within his own organization, a responsible leader is
respectful to those above him and reserved with those
beneath him. When dealing with outsiders, he is
calm and assured but careful when he speaks. When
working with lower-level employees, an effective
leader is pleasant and efficient. When working with
those higher in the organization, he is polite and unpretentious. When summoned by the highest managers, he is confident but formal. Strength of
personality counts for only so much. Manners and
appearance command respect in the long run only
when a leader is capable of carrying out his tasks.
The criterion of leadership is the ability to think
clearly and work hard rather than to look good.*

At the beginning of 1940, Dwight Eisenhower was a
nearly 50-year-old lieutenant colonel in the U.S. Army.
In his own opinion, his prospects for promotion to the
rank of one-star (brigadier) general were "nil." Yet, only
two years later, he had been promoted to four-star general and was in command of the greatest invasion force
ever created. Describing Ike's rise as "meteoric" is a
decided understatement. Although it is easy for us to
justify in hindsight his rapid promotion because of his
subsequent successes as the Allied Supreme Commander, what did the men responsible for his promotion have to go on? What factors did General George C.
Marshall, the Army's Chief of Staff, and President

Franklin Roosevelt use in selecting Eisenhower over scores of otherwise well qualified Army officers available at the time? Four factors made Eisenhower stand out from the crowd and pointed to his superior ability to lead people and get the job done.

First, Eisenhower had prepared himself for the challenge. In the 1920s, Eisenhower had served under Major General Fox Conner in Panama. General Conner was an extremely able and knowledgeable officer. He had been General Pershing's operations officer in France during World War I. Conner's study of history led him to believe that another war with Germany was inevitable. He believed that this war would be fought by a coalition of western allies and could only be won if the western allies were under a unified command. Eisenhower took Conner's beliefs to heart and developed himself to be a leader in that command. For example, he acquired and studied books on Luxembourg, Belgium, and the Low Countries. When asked by an associate why he had these books, he replied that these countries were "where the next war was going to be fought and I intend to know more about them than anyone else."

Second, he passed the test of performance on a personal level. A superior described Eisenhower as "[a] man possessing broad vision, progressive ideas, a thorough grasp of the magnitude of problems involved in handling an army, and lots of initiative and resourcefulness." General Douglas MacArthur called Eisenhower, who served as MacArthur's aide in the

Philippines during the 1930s, the best officer in the Army. But it was General George Marshall who selected Eisenhower to command the European theater. In his biography *Eisenhower*, Steven Ambrose wrote of Marshall's decision: "For six months, [Marshall] had been in daily, often hourly, contact with Eisenhower. He had given Eisenhower broad responsibilities and a wide scope. Not once had Eisenhower let him down. Marshall appreciated the manner in which Eisenhower accepted responsibility and, even more, Eisenhower's offensive-mindedness, his calm confidence that if the Allies made an all-out effort they could successfully invade France . . . The major factor in Marshall's thinking, however, was simple and direct. After the war, speaking of Eisenhower's promotion, Marshall commented, 'If he hadn't delivered he wouldn't have moved up.' "

Third, Eisenhower clearly understood the requirements of leadership during a war. Ambrose continued: "Eisenhower felt that the Army needed strong, tough, efficient, hardworking officers to meet the demands . . . Too many officers who had done their jobs well, even brilliantly, in peacetime, did not measure up under wartime conditions. They could not take the physical or mental strain of combat. One reason Eisenhower drove his unit so hard was to find out which of his officers could still make sound logical decisions and see to it their orders were carried out when the officers had gone for days with little sleep, no hot food, no relief from the constant stress of making and enforcing decisions."

Eisenhower felt that certain characteristics were unsuited to those who held high command positions. He wrote that "long and bitter wars . . . send to the bone piles those that . . . indulge in petty jealousies, personal animosities, and the like; they bring to the top the fellow who thinks more of [doing] his job than of his own promotion prospects. The nervous energy and drive that are required in bringing a large unit along to high training standards is tremendous; only people who are highly trained professionally and who have an inexhaustible supply of determination can get away with it. Professional military ability and strength of character, always required in high military position, are often marred by unfortunate characteristics, the two most frequently encountered and hurtful being too obvious avidity for public acclaim and the delusion that strength of purpose demands arrogant and even insufferable deportment." Eisenhower himself provided the example. He worked eighteen hours a day, seven days a week when necessary. When something needed to be done, he unfailingly did it, but in a way that was acceptable to those around him.

Finally, Eisenhower created high morale, enthusiasm, and cooperation in his troops and among his peers. Ambrose wrote: "He was concerned with morale, did all he could to build it up and keep it high. He was convinced that 'Americans either will not or cannot fight at maximum efficiency unless they understand the why and wherefore of their orders,' so wherever he went he talked, asked questions, listened, observed. He was patient, clear and logical in his explanations to his officers and men about why things had to be done this way or that. He mingled with the men on an informal basis, got to know them, listened to their gripes, and, when appropriate, did something about them. He believed that 'morale is the strongest and most delicate of growths. It withstands shocks, even disasters of the battlefield, but can be destroyed utterly by favoritism, neglect, or injustice.' " In addition to recognizing Eisenhower's technical competence, people liked and trusted him because they perceived him as fair and just. He did not threaten, intimidate, or abuse those around him, and, as a result, they willingly followed him.

XIII
Knowledge

Knowledge: The foundation of successful leadership. Knowledge has three aspects. The first, *fundamental knowledge*, deals with studying science, history, and human nature; in other words, learning the basics of the art of leadership. The second, *strategic knowledge*, concerns understanding the needs and goals of both constituents and competitors and planning effective operations to reach objectives. The third, *tactical knowledge*, focuses on uncovering evolving threats and opportunities and responding swiftly and appropriately to them, within the strategic framework, through innovation and improvisation.

Ulysses S. Grant: Facing the Unknown

The first quality of a leader is great knowledge. Knowledge does not come from intuition, but is the result of study and experience. A man is not born a leader. He must become one. Not to be anxious; to be always cool; to avoid confusion; to make appropriate decisions in the midst of confusion and chaos with as much composure as if he were perfectly at ease. These are proofs of knowledge. The central task in leading competitive operations is maintaining flexibility, a task most difficult to perform well. To do so requires overcoming the confusion, obscurity, and uncertainty peculiar to competitive situations and discovering the order, clarity, and certainty in them; only thus can opportunities be realized. Naturally, in the course of a business operation, one would like to fulfill the initial plan . . . but this is almost never possible. Therefore, ensure that both plans and resources are flexible and adaptable to circumstances. Your plans should foresee and provide for a next step in case of success, failure, or partial success—which is the most common case. Your attitude and your organization structure should allow exploitation of opportunity or adaptation to changing conditions in the shortest possible time. Activity provides information and generates opportunity. A leader should execute his carefully drawn plans with as little delay as possible. Benefiting from unforeseen opportunity is what cures problems and makes fortunes. Learn to profit from the immediate circumstances.

A leader must make a decision to act based on the information available at the time a decision is required. In most decision situations, a leader cannot know everything he needs to know in order to assure success. To a greater or lesser degree, a mist of uncertainty surrounds every decision. Hence, one of the greatest challenges to decision-making is fear of unpredictable or unintended results. Leaders cannot operate effectively in difficult situations unless they can master their fear of the unknown.

In the summer of 1861, at the beginning of the American Civil War, Ulysses S. Grant, who later defeated Robert E. Lee in Virginia and was elected President of the United States, was a colonel in command of a regiment of Union troops from Illinois, his native state.

When he was appointed to command the 21st Illinois Infantry regiment, Grant's qualifications for leadership were questionable. Grant attended West Point as a young man, graduating in 1843, and fought in the Mexican-American War under General Zachary Taylor. A large percentage of the general officers of both the Union and Confederate armies fought in this war, including Robert E. Lee. (Grant notes in his *Memoirs* that he met Lee briefly in Mexico. Lee, however, had no recollection of the meeting.) Grant was a commissary officer. He never commanded troops in battle. He resigned from the Army in July 1854 because he did not want to be separated from his wife. From 1854 to 1861, he tried and failed at farming, real estate, and selling firewood. Finally, in desperation, he went to work as a clerk in his brother's Galena, Illinois, leather store.

Given Grant's lack of experience in leading troops and his troops' lack of experience in fighting, it is not surprising that Grant felt both fear and anxiety over the stark prospect of a real battle when his regiment was ordered to attack a Confederate camp near the town of Florida, Missouri, commanded by Confederate Colonel Thomas Harris. In his *Memoirs*, he writes: "Harris had been encamped in a creek bottom for the sake of being close to water. The hills on either side of the creek extend to a considerable height, possibly more than a hundred feet. As we approached the brow of the hill from which it was expected we could see Harris' camp, and possibly find his men formed to meet us, my heart kept getting higher and higher until it felt to me as though it was in my throat. I would have given anything to be back in Illinois, but I had not the moral courage to halt and consider what to do; *I kept right on*. When we reached a point from which the valley below was in full view I halted. The place where Harris had been encamped a few days before was still there and marks of recent encampment were plainly visible, but the troops were gone. My heart resumed its place. *It occurred to me at once that Harris had been as much afraid of me as I had been of him.* This was a view of the question I had never taken before; but it was one I never forgot afterwards. From that event to the close of the war, I never experienced trepidation upon confronting an enemy, although I always felt more or less anxiety. I never forgot that he had as much reason to fear my forces as I had [to fear] his. The lesson was valuable." (Emphasis added.)

Major General J.F.C. Fuller commented on this passage in his book, *Grant and Lee: A Study in Personality and Generalship*: "The remarkable point in this confession is not that Grant overcame his fears and 'kept right on,' but that he analyzed his fears. For a brief moment fear mastered him, then he mastered fear, and having done so at once examined why it had mastered him. Having discovered the reason, he learned one of the most important lessons in generalship [and leadership], namely that he who fears the least holds the initiative, and that he who can make his adversary fear more than he does himself has already defeated [his adversary] morally."

It is perfectly natural for decisions made under conditions of uncertainty (as most decisions are) to cause anxiety and concern. A leader's ability to act in spite of his fear of failure determines whether he succeeds or fails. Everyone is afraid of the unknown. Those who "keep right on" will eventually win.

Thomas A. Edison: Leadership and Innovation

What is knowledge? To understand that you know something when you do, and to admit that you do

not know something when you do not. That is knowl-
edge. Seek understanding like a thirsty man lost in
the desert seeks water—with fearful determination.
Learn by observing the behavior of other people. If
you observe good behavior, copy it. If you observe
bad behavior, look for the same behavior in yourself
and eliminate it. Some people claim to have inher-
ited intuitive genius from their ancestors or their col-
lege professors. How fortunate for them! For those of
us who have not, however, the only alternative is to
listen carefully and observe closely. Knowledge and
experience, combined with study and reflection, will
have to substitute for our lack of genius.

The critical success factor in competitive leadership is
using innovation. In *The Art of War*, Sun Tzu says: "A
person uses normal or expected tactics to confront the
enemy. But it is the power of the unexpected, the innovative, which provides the opportunity for victory."
Effective innovation in an organization is a function of
the attitude of its leaders toward failure. Leaders must
support and encourage experimentation in order to obtain the benefits of innovation. Successful innovation is
based on experimental failure; the greater the tolerance
for experimentation in an organization, the greater the
opportunity to learn. Major innovations are not made in
great jumps, nor in blinding flashes of intuition; rather,
they evolve from incremental additions to already existing knowledge. Incremental additions to knowledge

are built on disciplined, directed (but not managed or controlled) experimentation.

The methods and attitudes employed by Thomas A. Edison to create thousands of small improvements and many major discoveries still stand as an outstanding model of the experimental process. In 1869, Edison, then 22 years old, arrived in New York from Boston, where he had just lost all his money backing an unsuccessful product he had developed. By 1871, two years later, he had established a laboratory in which he could work on developing products. Matthew Josephson, in his biography *Edison*, wrote:

"When the devices of others were brought to him for inspection, it was seldom that he could not contribute his own technical refinements or ideas for improved mechanical construction. As he worked over such machines, certain insights came to him; by dint of many trials, materials long known to others, construction long accepted, were 'put together in a different way'—and there you have an *invention*. This would follow usually upon an extended period of patient observation and testing that ended with some act of insight coming 'suddenly,' as it appeared, but in reality derived from an accumulated body of technical knowledge stored in the searcher's mind."

The path to successful innovation is neither straight nor short. Edison himself wrote: "It has been just so in all my inventions. The first step is intuition—and comes with a burst, then difficulties arise. [One] thing gives out and then [another]—'Bugs'—as such little faults and difficulties are called—show themselves . . . months of anxious watching, study, and labor are [required] before commercial success—or failure—is certainly reached . . . I may have the right principle and [be] on the right track, but time, hard work, and some good luck are necessary too . . . I would construct a theory and work on its lines until I found it untenable, then it would be discarded and another theory evolved. This was the only possible way for me to work out the problem . . ." Persistence is the key.

There are two great challenges to effective innovation in the workplace. The first challenge is the "not invented here" syndrome. (This is a close cousin of the "we never did it that way before" syndrome.) People usually believe that their own experiences in life form a sufficient basis for making judgments and decisions. The older and more experienced they become, the more they think they know how things really work. Hence, people have a tendency to reject ideas that did not originate with them. They want to do things in a comfortable, familiar way.

The second challenge is the "many minds are better than one" syndrome. Groupthink and committee decision-making in programs such as Total Quality Management is particularly destructive. Committees cannot come up with, nor deal with, original ideas, even if the committees are filled with intelligent, well-intentioned people. This is particularly true in highly bureaucratic organizations, where new ideas and methods are most desperately needed.

Edison's approach to innovation through experimentation created the light bulb, the phonograph, and numerous other devices. He often had several lines of investigation going at the same time. Copying his model for use in today's workplace will also produce great benefits. It is the responsibility of organizational leaders to provide an atmosphere of encouragement and support that will allow organizational members to experiment with ideas and learn from their failures. In this way, leaders can release the infinite power of innovation.

XIV
Laddership

Laddership: A leader understands the special nature of the social and moral contract between leaders and their constituents. The leader is dependent upon his followers for his power and, to a large extent, his ability to produce results. Therefore, he must work cooperatively with them to reach agreed-upon objectives. But, at the same time, strong leadership is one of the more important factors, if not the only absolutely necessary one, in the success of those human activities that depend upon cooperation. Therefore, a leader is charged with the responsibility of imposing, through the exercise of appropriate power, whatever level of order and discipline is required to meet objectives. He does this in part by using a system of rewards and penalties that is perceived as fair and just by his constituents.

Lawrence of Arabia: Encouraging Respect

If a person demands excellence from himself but much less from other people, he will have few difficulties in dealing with them. If you want to encourage mutual respect and teamwork in the workplace, always be courteous and considerate of others. Accomplishing worthwhile goals becomes easier when people respect each other and work harmoniously in teams. A leader can be called truly skillful in human relations when he values other people's strong points even after learning about their faults. An outstanding leader quickly overlooks small faults, errors, or wrongs. As a result, he has few enemies. Petty disagreements can disrupt team spirit, just as small irritations and minor impatience can destroy great projects. The personal competence of a single individual alone is not decisive, but rather the combined competence of all members of an organization. The latter rests on the good opinion and the confidence each individual member places in the unit to which he belongs. The least effective members of an organization, if banded together appropriately, have their power. Solidarity and confidence in the face of pressure cannot be improvised; they must be learned over time. Many people think that it is incorrect application of organizational behavior theories that creates strained relations between executives and employees. Strained relations are a matter of basic attitude, of executives and employees lacking mutual respect. The habit of talking down to employees is one of the worst vices that can afflict an executive. The value of tact cannot be overemphasized. Do not look down on others because you outrank them. Encourage and listen well to the words of your subordinates. It is well known that the most valuable minerals lie hidden in the ground.

Allied strategy for defeating Germany in World War I depended, in part, on the British defeating the Turks in the Middle East. The Arab armies were instrumental in providing needed support to the main British army. British officers who spoke Arabic were assigned to the Arab army as advisors. One of these officers was Captain (later Lieutenant Colonel) T. E. Lawrence, better known as Lawrence of Arabia. Lawrence served with the Arabs, fighting a bitter, difficult guerrilla war in the desert. His success during this period was based in large measure on his understanding of the Arab culture and his ability to be accepted by his constituents, the Arab men who comprised his fighting units and the Arab leaders who commanded them.

In August 1917, Lawrence wrote a summary of his rules for dealing effectively with the Arabs. He called the summary "Twenty-seven Articles." It was published in the "Arab Bulletin," a newsletter of sorts containing military information useful to British officers fighting in Arabia. In its original form, the advice given was specifically directed toward officers serving in Arabia; but any leader would be well served by following it, providing he has the self-discipline to do so. Here is a synopsis of "Twenty-seven Articles" (slightly altered for modern readers):

1. Go easy in the beginning. A bad start is difficult to overcome. Most people make judgments based on relatively minor aspects of behavior and attitude.

2. Learn all you can about your associates. Get to know their concerns, friends, enemies, ideas, requirements, and biases. Learn by listening. Speak their language, not your own.

3. Respect your unit commanders. Deal with them directly on matters of importance. Never go around your subordinates.

4. Win and keep the confidence of your supporters. Do not discourage ideas, but make sure you can control the outcome of events.

5. Remain in communication with your group.

6. Do not get too close to your subordinates. Disclosing your weaknesses through familiarity only serves to undermine your authority.

7. Hold yourself above the level of your subordinates and the subordinates of your peers. Precedence is a serious matter in most organizations, so put yourself on the highest level possible.

8. The ideal position is when you are able to lead without being intrusive. Do not become too in-

timate, too prominent, or too earnest. Maintain prestige and control.

9. Magnify your image and that of your fellow executives. Assure that the merit of leaders is well known.

10. Show respect when addressing leaders. Be somewhat distant, although polite, with lower-level individuals.

11. An outsider is generally not popular with people. When you must, keep a strongly based insider in front of you as a shield.

12. Cling tightly to your sense of humor.

13. Never argue or display negative emotions in public; you may degrade yourself.

14. People are generally difficult to drive, but easy to lead, if you have patience with them.

15. Do not try to do too much yourself. It is better to allow people to do their own work reasonably well than for you to do it for them perfectly, even assuming you can.

16. A well-placed compliment is the most effective way to win someone over. Always repay a good deed in kind. But do not fawn over people; they will lose respect for you.

17. Dress in the manner preferred by your customers and superiors.

18. Leaders are like actors on a stage. To be successful requires constant attention to the part you are playing.

19. Wear and use the best. Clothes and accessories are important tokens of status.

20. Adopt the customs of those you intend to influence.

21. People are heavily attached to their biases. Avoid criticism.

22. Your constituents have their own ways of solving problems and dealing with situations generally learned through experience. Take the best from their methods and use it in combination with the best from yours.

23. When objections to your ideas are raised by your constituents, be sure you understand the reasoning behind these objections completely. People will not necessarily tell you everything they are thinking. Get to the root of the problem.

24. Do not ask people with differing philosophies, backgrounds, and work ethics to mix together effectively.

25. Keep your personal life personal.

26. Choose your closest associates carefully. They are reflections of your judgment and character for all to see.

27. The beginning and the end of the secret of leading people is constant study of them. Keep always on your guard; never say an unnecessary thing. Watch yourself and your associates at all times. Hear all that passes; search out what is going on beneath the surface. Read character;

discover weakness and strength; seek understanding, but keep what you learn to yourself.
Bury yourself in the concerns of your constituents, have no interests and no ideas except the
work at hand. Your success will be apportioned
according to the amount of mental effort you
devote to it.

George Washington: Political Wisdom

*When there is no one in control, no leader, nothing
useful or distinguished or profitable can be accomplished. This is true of all aspects of life, and especially true where competitive business is concerned.
In competitive business, leadership vision combined
with cooperative action is the only way to produce
favorable results. An essential element in understanding the nature of leadership is that a leader
works with thinking, feeling people. These people are
afraid of failure, and suffer from anxiety, jealousy,
disease, and fatigue. Some are ambitious, some are
not. Some are competent, others are dull. Some are
cooperative and loyal, others insubordinate and superficial. In short, they carry within themselves a
thousand and one differences. To make them perform
as a team, it is not enough for a leader to decide what
should be done and issue the orders for carrying out
his intentions. He must also create a spirit of confidence in those under him. Confidence is the foundation of success in business: each person's belief*

in his own competence, and his trust in the competence of other members of his group. Senior executives who complain about the low morale of their employees evidently do not realize that employee morale is a mirror of confidence in their leadership. Confidence in leaders is an integral element of organizational spirit.

Leaders must develop wisdom in order to understand the best way to serve the total needs of their constituents. Serving the total needs of a constituency requires a thorough understanding of human nature coupled with knowledge of the current situation and a good feel for the implications and potential complications associated with various courses of action.

In January 1777, George Washington was camped in the hills around Morristown, New Jersey, after winning the Battles of Trenton and Princeton. The British were bottled up in New York City for the time being.

General Washington, however, faced a serious problem. The British strategy for winning the Revolutionary War was based on gaining control of one section of the thirteen colonies at a time. The plan was for the British army to recapture an area. After recapture, armed militia composed of people who were loyal to England (Tories) would hold territory for the crown. As the British marched through New Jersey, they offered immunity to anyone who would swear allegiance to England. The British believed that once people were "liberated" from the threat of harm from rebel forces, they would again be loyal to their "natural" country, England. Of course, a large number of people immediately came forward to swear loyalty to England so that they would be able to retain their homes and farms. But now that the Continental Army was in control of New Jersey, Washington had to determine the fate of the people who went over to the British during their occupation of New Jersey.

There were several factors to consider. On one hand, the British were considered the enemy. People who collaborated with them were considered traitors by the hard-liners. Revolutionary passions demanded that they be punished. On the other hand, Washington needed the cooperation of the people of the region for supplies and information. His army would not survive long if he turned his own people against him.

Washington decided that tolerance was the best approach. He issued a proclamation that allowed persons who had sworn loyalty to the British to present themselves to the nearest military headquarters and swear allegiance to the United States. All would be forgiven. If a person presented himself but did not wish to swear allegiance to the United States, and had not committed any act of war against the Continental Army, he would be escorted unharmed to the British lines. Furthermore, his family would be allowed to retain their lands and possessions.

Washington's purpose in taking this action was twofold. First, he did not want to create any martyrs. People killed in retribution for swearing loyalty to England would serve as focal points for anti-Continental sentiment. They would be used by the British as examples of rebel brutality. Second, the conditions in British-held New York City were miserable. Food and housing were in short supply. The majority of food and housing went to the British army. Colonial Tories received the remainder, which was not very much, nor very good. Furthermore, the British treated the colonials with contempt. For the most part, conditions were far better out in the country than in the city.

Washington's solution to this problem had three beneficial effects. First, a large number of the people of New Jersey were not polarized against the revolutionary cause. Because of his generous treatment, Washington gave no one an opportunity to attack him for cruelty or intolerance after the war was over. Second, those people who sought refuge with the British suffered at the hands of their "friends." This served to convince a number of them that the British were not really friends after all. Third, Washington's reputation for fairness and wisdom was greatly enhanced. Had he not acted from an understanding of human nature and a knowledge of the consequences of his actions, he might very well have laid the groundwork for subsequent military and political failure.

XV
Example

Example: A leader's actions become a model for the actions of his constituent group. Further, the leader's character sets the moral tone of leadership. The standards he uses become the benchmarks for the group. The people he favors become his flag-bearers. In all situations, the leader is observed and copied; at all times, the leader demonstrates preferred or ideal behavior by his own actions. The leader sets the example whether he intends to or not!

Robert E. Lee: A Model for Honor and Glory

Essential to leadership is to share the rewards and problems of subordinates. If you encounter difficulties, do not abandon your group to save yourself, do not seek personal escape from the challenges con-

fronting you. Rather, make every effort to protect your subordinates and associates, sharing their fate. If you do this, your constituents will not forget you. What is the truest test of human character? It is probably this: that a person will know how to be patient in the midst of hard circumstance, and can continue to be personally effective while living through whatever discouragements beset him and his associates. One should not carry malice in his heart. If a malicious person is in a high position, his constituents will fight among themselves continuously. Civility is both rational and farsighted, for it endows the person who displays it with a sense of superiority and encourages cooperation among people. The actions of executives are like the wind, while those of employees are like the grass. When the wind blows, the grass bends in the same direction.

General Robert E. Lee's successes in leading the Army of Northern Virginia during the American Civil War are well known. He is considered one of the greatest military minds in history. But Lee's greatest service to the people of the State of Virginia and the South may have occurred after the Civil War was over.

Defeat was bitter for General Lee. Lee liked to win; the old warrior believed passionately in his cause, the defense of the State of Virginia. At the Battle of Fredericksburg, in December 1862, in the midst of one of the greatest Confederate victories, Lee said to General James Longstreet, "It is well that war is so terrible— lest we should grow too fond of it!" At Appomattox

EXAMPLE   169

Courthouse in 1865 when he realized that surrender was inevitable, Lee said, "There is nothing left for me to do but go and see General Grant and I would rather die a thousand deaths. How easily I could get rid of this [burden] and be at rest! I have only to ride along the lines and all will be over. But, it is our duty to live— for what will become of the women and children of the South if we are not here to support and protect them?"

In August 1865, Washington College (now Washington and Lee University) in Lexington, Virginia, offered Lee the position of president of the college. Lee hesitated to accept this position because he did not know if he could fulfill the requirements of the job and he was afraid his notoriety would damage the reputation of the school. In a letter to the trustees of the college, he wrote:

"Being excluded from the terms of the amnesty in the proclamation of President of the United States, of the 29th of May last, and an object of censure to a portion of the country, I have thought it probable that my occupation of the position of president might draw upon the college a feeling of hostility; and I should therefore cause injury to an institution which it would be my highest desire to advance. I think it is the duty of every citizen, in the present condition of the country, to do all in his power to aid in the restoration of peace and harmony, and in no way to oppose the policy of the State or General Government, directed to that object. It is particularly incumbent on those charged with the instruction of the young to set them an example of submission to authority, and I could not consent to be the cause of animadversion upon the college.

"Should you, however, take a different view, and think that my services in the position tendered to me by the Board will be advantageous to the college and country, I will yield to your judgment, and accept it; otherwise I must most respectfully decline the office."

The trustees of Washington College insisted that Lee take the presidency. Many people wondered why Lee would accept this particular position. He had other offers that would have made him a wealthy man. For example, one New York insurance firm is rumored to have offered him a million dollars (remember, in 1865, a million dollars was **really** a million dollars) just to name him president of the company and use his name in promoting their services. Lee declined this offer. Further, Washington College was in a state of physical and financial disarray from the war. Other, more prestigious institutions would have been glad to have Lee serve as president. So why did he select Washington College?

It was his desire to give an example of service to the people of the South. In his own words, "I have a self-imposed task, which I must accomplish. I have led the young men of the South in battle; I have seen many of them fall under my standard. I shall devote my life now to training young men to do their duty in life."

Lee believed that empowering his students was the best preparation for a responsible life. Rather than promulgate a body of rules for the students (many of whom were hardened veterans of the Civil War), he

EXAMPLE   171

simply set the expectation that "each student always conduct himself as a gentleman." If this expectation was not met, a student would find himself face to face with Lee behind the closed door of the president's office . . . a highly undesirable fate! Students followed the rules at Washington College because they did not want to disappoint Lee. Empowerment succeeded because Lee governed his own behavior with the same strictness he demanded of his students.

Robert E. Lee's five-year tenure as president of Washington College was a complete success. He rebuilt the college from the ruin of war into a fine institution. Some of the innovations he installed at Washington College were copied at other schools throughout the country. After his death, he was described by a colleague as not only the finest general ever produced in America, but also the finest college president.

Lee's philosophy, for which he served as a living example both on the battlefield and in the classroom, was "There is true glory and a true honor: the glory of duty done—the honor of integrity of principle. Public and private life are subject to the same rules; and truth and responsibility will carry you through this world much better than policy, or tact, or expediency, or any other word that was devised to conceal, or mystify a deviation from a straight line."

George Washington: Commitment to Principle

It is proper for persons of great ability and high ambition to strive for wealth and power. But do not deceive yourself about these things! Wealth and power gained by forfeiting the principles underlying your character cannot possibly bring you contentment. Moreover, how can you claim to be an example for others to follow if you ignore your own principles— even if only for a little while? After all, a petty thief does exactly the same thing. Encourage people to strive for excellence by striving for excellence yourself. Lead by example! Character is the bedrock on which the whole edifice of leadership rests. With character, the full worth of the individual and his team can be realized. Without it, failure or, at best, mediocrity will result. Character is a habit. It is created through the daily choice of right and wrong. It is a moral quality which grows gradually to maturity. It does not appear suddenly. Your organization is a reflection of yourself. By greatness of character, an executive gains command over himself. By consistency and competence, he gains the respect of his subordinates. The success of the entire group is based on the firmness of the conduct of the executive who will manage it. An executive should be professional in his attitudes, naturally suited for command, profound in his thinking, sound in his judgment, hard-

EXAMPLE   173

*working, and emotionally stable. He should instill
respect in his subordinates through an appropriate
system of rewards and penalties. He should be kind,
gracious, and civil under most circumstances, but
stern when necessary. Above all, an executive must
be judged by his actions, and it is preferable that he
be chosen for command on the basis of his example.*

By early 1783, the Revolutionary War was all but over.
A preliminary peace treaty had been signed in Paris in
November 1782. But the battle for independence and
freedom was not finished. In March 1783, the greatest
enemy of independence and freedom was not Britain,
but rather the very soldiers who fought the Revolutionary War. It is in this battle that George Washington,
through his example, made one of his greater contributions as a leader.

The thirteen colonies were, in 1783, bound together
in a loose alliance governed by the Articles of Confederation, a document that preceded the Constitution.
The Articles of Confederation did not recognize the ex-
istence of a "federal" government, nor did they provide
the Continental Congress with the power to raise
money or to collect taxes. Any money available to the
Continental Congress to supply the Continental Army
and pay the troops was provided on an almost voluntary
basis by the thirteen states. Further, the Continental
Congress had issued currency and debt to finance the
war. At the end of the Revolutionary War, no money
was left to pay the army or the debts. The states were
increasingly reluctant to provide funds, because the cri-

sis had passed. Hence, the currency was worthless; the debts uncollectible.

For members of the army, particularly the officers, the Continental Congress's lack of funds created a desperate situation. The Continental Congress owed large amounts to the army for back pay and pensions that had been promised to induce these men to serve. But it quickly became obvious to the soldiers that the army was going to be dissolved without the promised amounts being paid, leaving many of them destitute. As a result, some of the more powerful army officers, assisted by powerful civilian money interests (who were holding much of the now worthless currency and debt), began to talk about using the army to force the state legislatures to pay the amounts owed. In effect, the army was threatening to overthrow the weak and disorganized government of the United States.

The conspirators knew that George Washington would be a great asset in overthrowing the government if they could convince him that it was the right move. Alexander Hamilton and others presented arguments to Washington that implied that the only course of action available to save the country from anarchy was to use the army to temporarily seize power. If Washington were to lead the army in this action, argued Hamilton and others, then there would be minimal bloodshed and disruption. Once the army had been paid, they said, the government would be returned to civilian control. At this moment, the future of American democracy hung in the balance.

EXAMPLE   175

After considerable thought, Washington rejected this approach. Washington wrote, in reply to a letter suggesting he consider becoming king of the United States: "No occurrence in the course of the war has given me more painful sensations than your information that such ideas exist in the Army. I must view them with abhorrence . . . I am at a loss to conceive what part of my conduct could have given encouragement to an [idea] which to me seems [filled] with the greatest mischiefs which can befall my Country."

But the idea that the army needed to overthrow the government would not die. A greatly concerned Washington called a meeting of army officers at his Newburgh, New York, headquarters on March 15, 1783. This meeting was one of the most important meetings in the short history of the United States of America. The meeting's outcome would determine the fate of the future government of the United States.

Washington's carefully prepared speech for this meeting argued that overthrowing the government was counterproductive and would only serve to hurt the families and friends of the soldiers themselves. He appealed to the higher ideals of the revolution and to patriotism. He assured the men that the Congress would eventually give them just compensation and that he would personally fight to see justice done. Washington's arguments failed to convince the men. They remained determined to take action.

In desperation, Washington tried to read another letter that he hoped would sway the officers. But the handwriting on the letter was too small for his vision. He reached into his pocket and pulled out his eyeglasses. As he put the glasses on, Washington said, "I hope you gentlemen will pardon me. I have not only become gray in serving my country, but it seems I am also going blind." This simple, humble statement, which embodied the commitment and sacrifice that George Washington personally represented, changed the outcome of the meeting. In response to Washington's example, the men decided to wait for Congress to act and allow Washington to plead their case before Congress. Thomas Jefferson later said, "The moderation and virtue exemplified by Washington's character alone prevented this revolution from ending, as most others have, by subverting the liberty it was intended to establish."